THE blues

roots and inspiration

THE blues

roots and inspiration

john collis

PUBLISHED BY

SALAMANDER BOOKS LIMITED

LONDON

A SALAMANDER BOOK

Published by Salamander Books Ltd
129–137 York Way, London N7 9LG
United Kingdom

This edition distributed by
SMITHMARK Publishers,
a division of U.S. Media Holdings, Inc.,
115 West 18th Street, New York NY 10011

9 8 7 6 5 4 3 2 1

SMITHMARK Books are available for bulk purchase
for sales promotion and premium use. For details
write or call the manager of special sales,
SMITHMARK Publishers,
115 West 18th Street, New York NY 10011
(212) 532-6600

ISBN 0-8317-6259-4

Printed in Italy

Credits
Editor: Alice Duke
Designer: Paul Johnson
Picture Research: Alice Duke
Map: Janos Marffy (© Salamander Books Ltd)
Color reproduction: Classic Scan, Singapore

Acknowledgements by the author
The scope of this book, essentially an extended,
illustrated essay, demanded that some stern
decisions be made at the outset. Since it was
obviously going to be necessary to stride fairly
briskly along the main highways of the blues,
resisting the temptation to wander too far down
alleyways or linger in one spot, it has been written
as an overall survey of the subject, perhaps as an
introduction aimed at the new convert to the
excitement of the blues, or for someone with a
more general interest in popular music.

Of course the blues is 'important'. Not only is it,
with Hollywood cinema, one of America's most
significant contributors to contemporary culture,
but its roots in slavery, and its development
through diaspora from the American South, make
it of historical, sociological and moral, as well as
musical, interest. However, the sociologist and
historian can sometimes write about popular
music with a dead hand: this book has, I hope,
been informed by the enthusiasm of one who
could not imagine going a week without the
company of Jimmy Reed or John Lee Hooker.

The perspective is my own, informed by a forty-
year love affair with this music, but naturally my
ideas over the years have also been guided by
distinguished researchers into the subject. Three
books that I first read in the 1960s deserve
particular mention: *The Country Blues* by Samuel
B. Charters (Rinehart & Co Inc, 1959), *Urban
Blues* by Charles Keil (University of Chicago Press,
1966) and *The Story of the Blues* by Paul Oliver
(Barrie & Jenkins, 1969). The last of these is
currently being updated.

In addition, the following books are the ones that
I regularly consulted:
Oakley, Giles, *The Devil's Music*, BBC, 1976.
Springer, Robert, *Authentic Blues: Its History and
Its Themes*, Edwin Mellen Press, 1995.
Oliver, Paul, (edited by) *The Blackwell Guide to
Recorded Blues*, Blackwell, 1989.
Oliver, Paul, *Savannah Syncopators: African
Retentions in the Blues*, Studio Vista, 1970.
Leadbitter, Mike and Slaven, Neil, *Blues Records
1943–1966*, Hanover Books, 1968.
Brunning, Bob, *Blues in Britain*, Blandford, 1995.
Bastin, Bruce, *Red River Blues*, The Macmillan
Press Ltd, 1986.
Dixon, Willie and Snowdon, Don, *I Am the Blues*,
Quartet, 1989.
Broven, John, *Walking to New Orleans*, Blues
Unlimited, 1974.
Collis, John, (edited by), *The Rock Primer*, Penguin,
1980.

When there is conflicting evidence about birth
dates and career details, I have almost invariably
gone along with my main reference source,
Sheldon Harris's monumental *Blues Who's Who*
(Arlington House, 1979). *The Faber Companion to
20th Century Popular Music* by Phil Hardy and
Dave Laing, and *The Penguin Encyclopedia of
Popular Music*, edited by Donald Clarke, were also
a great help.

My grateful thanks are extended to all these
writers, to Tony Russell for kindly suggesting that
I should write the book, to Alice Duke of
Salamander Books Ltd., and above all, to the
bluesmen who have excited, moved and
entertained me for most of my life. In particular
to Bo Diddley, to whom this book is respectfully
dedicated.

CONTENTS

map

MAINE

_____ VERMONT
NEW HAMPSHIRE
MASSACHUSETTS
RHODE ISLAND
CONNECTICUT

NEW JERSEY

DELAWARE
DISTRICT OF COLUMBIA
MARYLAND

NEW YORK

New York

PENNSYLVANIA
Philadelphia
Pittsburgh
Baltimore

WEST
RGINIA   Richmond

VIRGINIA

NORTH
CAROLINA
Charlotte

Greenville
SOUTH
CAROLINA
Charleston
Statesboro
acon

EORGIA

FLORIDA
Tampa

Main map: Features towns and cities that have been significant in the history of the blues.

Inset map: This shows "the cradle of Delta blues", the area of land between the Mississippi River and one of its tributaries, the Yazoo, that became known as the Mississippi Delta.

TENNESSEE
ARKANSAS   Memphis
Little Rock

Yahoo River

Clarksdale

Delta

Greenville

MISSISSIPPI

Vicksburg
LOUISIANA   Jackson

Natchez

Mississippi River

Baton Rouge

New Orleans

in the beginning

"There's a great big mystery
And it surely is worrying me
This diddie wa diddie
This diddie wa diddie
I wish somebody would tell me what diddie wa diddie means"

From 'Diddie Wa Diddie' by Blind Blake

This book is a search for Blind Blake's "diddie wa diddie". Sometimes the blues is fear: "death is awful, spare me over another year"; sometimes it is jealousy, as in Roosevelt Sykes's graphic line: "I hate to think about another man snoring in my baby's face"; sometimes it is sexual boasting as in Muddy Waters's 'Hoochie Coochie Man'; sometimes it is a sense of restlessness: "I woke up this mornin', feelin' 'round for my shoes," sang Robert Johnson, "know 'bout 'at I got these old walkin' blues." It is also about hard times, poverty and racism; about the "strange fruit" of lynch-mob victims hanging from the trees; and of a defiant escape from oppression, even if only temporarily in dance and drink.

In the final years of the last century the legendary New Orleans cornet player and pioneer jazz-band leader, Buddy Bolden, was including in his repertoire tunes that we would now recognize as blues. In 1912 Hart Wand wrote his 'Dallas Blues', the first published song to use the word in its title, the sheet music for which went into a third edition within months. A year later W.C.Handy, self-styled "father of the blues", published his celebrated 'St Louis Blues', and in 1920, as the commercial recording industry was finding its feet,

Left: Ma Rainey and her Georgia Jazz Band. This celebrated
photograph was taken in 1923, the year Ma Rainey signed
with Paramount. By this time she was thirty-eight years old
and had already been performing for twenty-five years.

Right: The main vehicles for the blues were the traveling circuses, the minstrel shows and the similar "medicine shows", so-called because their purpose was to sell quack remedies. (The celebrated Rabbit Foot Minstrels, for example, were a vehicle for advertising a hair-straightening preparation.) These itinerant entertainments, which pre-dated Emancipation (Lincoln's Proclamation of Emancipation, signed in 1863), grew apace in the second half of the nineteenth century, and were musical and comic revues presenting a somewhat "Uncle Tom" vision of black American life.

Mamie Smith gave the emerging sound its first hit with 'Crazy Blues'.

And yet there is an irony in this progression. Bolden was not a bluesman. It seems more likely from the later testimony of musicians such as Bunk Johnson that he was building a bridge between ragtime and that other new musical style, jazz, and such testimony is all we have to go on, because as far as we know he never recorded (with the possible exception of a lost wax cylinder). Hart Wand was a white man from Oklahoma City who soon established a business in New Orleans manufacturing stationery items and never wrote another song, let alone a hit to match 'Dallas Blues'. W.C.Handy was indeed black, but he came from a comparatively well-off Memphis family and ran a sophisticated dance orchestra, a long way from the cotton fields (his strongest feeling for the blues, it would seem, was a desire to exploit the music commercially having noted its appeal to his audiences during the "interval spots" in which it was featured) and

Mamie Smith was a vaudeville entertainer, billed on her first record as "Mamie Smith, contralto".

These are curious staging posts in a journey we more usually think of as traveling from Africa to the rural South of the USA, before extending onwards and outwards to the clubs of Chicago and other industrial cities. Furthermore, it is a journey epitomized by a man with a guitar, whether it be Mance Lipscomb in farm denims or B.B.King in tuxedo and cummerbund. And yet, as the music became the rage of the 1920s, it was more typically performed in the city theatres by glamorous divas building on Mamie Smith's success. The discovery that the male-dominated blues of the countryside – a living folk music rather than a novelty jazz style – had immense commercial appeal was to come later, and somewhat belatedly.

It seems a reasonable assumption, an obvious one even, that the roots of the blues, the music of black America, lie in Africa. For 300 years, from the sixteenth century until the

American Civil War (1861–5), slaves were forcibly transported from there to the southern states. Although the vile trade was officially brought to an end in 1807, this ruling was simply ignored or by-passed by the European slave traders and their customers, both in the plantations and in the construction industries of the Caribbean and the American South.

In spite of this logical link with Africa it is hard to discern echoes of that continent's tribal music in the blues. There are, I believe, several reasons for this: firstly, there is a temptation to think of African music as a single, if unfocused, entity when of course there is no such thing – across the continent a rich variety of tribal musics is to be found; secondly, there is a feeling that slaves came from Africa as a whole, when in fact the majority came from the tribes of West Africa, particularly those of the coastal regions (it would have been decidedly uneconomical to risk transporting them around the

Cape, when each Atlantic crossing already incurred hundreds of deaths thanks to the appalling conditions on the slave ships).

In his book *Savannah Syncopators: African Retentions in the Blues*, Paul Oliver has sharpened the focus even further, citing the sub-Saharan savannah belt as the area where faint echoes of the blues can best be heard. In West Africa there was a long-established tradition of solo musicians, professional performers known as *griots*, whose position in some societies was an honored one. While this was not necessarily true of the itinerant blues entertainers of the rural South in the 1930s, a functional, if not a musical, similarity can be discerned. They traveled; they entertained; they were paid.

A third reason why African music is barely discernible in the compositions of the early blues singers is that the slave masters rigorously destroyed all aspects of African culture that might have posed a threat. Tribal drumming,

Left: Seen here playing the cornet, songwriter, bandleader, and publisher, W.C. Handy was one of the first to include "blue" notes (flattened thirds and sevenths) in a published composition. The self-proclaimed "father of the blues" is reputed to have referred to the music as "primitive", but is nevertheless important in that he helped to establish it formally.

Below: Ida Cox was the epitome of the "classic" blues woman. Stylish and independent, she was billed by Paramount as the "Uncrowned Queen of the Blues".

which could have contained coded communications, and any rituals that appeared to perpetuate the slaves' distinct identity were obvious targets, as were manufactured objects with a religious or cult significance, as in voodoo. What did survive, however, because it could not be physically broken, and was in any case seen to

have a function in helping to coordinate repetitive group work, was the specific tradition of 'call and response' singing. So it is here, in the work songs of the plantations and the chain gangs, that those faint echoes of Africa begin to resound.

A fourth reason is that several generations passed between the abolition of slavery and the growth of the record industry in the 1920s. Moreover, while it is on records that we can trace the development of the blues, it was at least two decades after the invention of the gramophone in 1887 that these became a ordinary commodity.

Finally, let us not forget that these African-Americans were merely one cultural mass in a vast country peopled almost entirely by immigrants. Europeans, for example, in particular the economic migrants from Celtic countries where music plays such a significant role in cultural identity, were also developing their indigenous music styles to suit the New World, and the countries of South America had a similarly fertile tradition. To put it simply, the blues musicians had distant roots in Africa, but their music was American, as American as ragtime, jazz or country and western.

There is an alternative view to the uniquely American nature of the music, albeit with African echoes, that sees it simply as a sub-category of the parent African tradition, particularly that of agrarian tribes; and since the pioneer folklorist Alan Lomax tended to this view, it must be respected. Perhaps we can agree that, in the decades since his field work in the 1930s and '40s, the blues has learned to stand on its own two feet, far away from the cultivated plains of West Africa.

Ironically, the end of slavery did little to improve social or economic conditions for black people. While the American Civil War may have freed them, it also ruined the economy of the defeated South; and of course it did nothing either to eradicate racial bigotry or to equip former slaves to fend for themselves. Your memory need only stretch back as far as the 1960s, a hundred years after that war, to recall enforced integration in schools and restaurants, the activities of the Klu Klux Klan, the Civil Rights

marches, and the Black Power movement. And you need no memory at all to know that American prisons and death rows are disproportionately populated by blacks, not because they are genetically less law-abiding, but because the law is more disposed to convict them. The struggle continues, and it is a struggle that has always been mirrored in the mainstream of black music. The road to gangsta rap began with the blues.

While early slave music was probably communal – largely hymns and work songs – the development of field hollers paved the way for the lone bluesman. These could be used not just for communication and for orchestrating physical effort, but as a solo performance, a private consolation, the musical expression of real experience. Emancipation, the breaking up of the slave gangs, would have had the effect of stressing the individualistic element in black culture. Gradually its songs became a mesh of borrowings, embellishments, and re-workings, as well as original expression.

And so, whereas hymns and spirituals were sung communally and therefore had to be standardized, the blues was more suited to a developing society of individuals. To a man walking behind his mule, ploughing a shallow furrow in arid dirt, the blues might be his only comfort. This is not to romanticize such hard labor – it has no romance even when carried out by a "free man" – but to suggest that the prevailing conditions were right for nurturing a new form of music: solo, inspirational, tailored to the singer's experience, bemoaning bad times and providing catharsis – the blues.

If jazz was born of the brass military instruments abandoned on a Civil War battlefield, the blues came into being when that field was tilled by a lone sharecropper, a poor individual who sought to use his music as a means of escape from that field and needed an instrumental accompaniment to do it. Initially this might have been a banjo or a violin, but neither instrument was ideal. The curt, rhythmic sound of the banjo might well have inspired the syncopations of ragtime but lacked the expressiveness and suppleness needed for the blues, and the violin

could only alternate with the voice rather than interweave with it. Whereas the rural bluesman's city cousin could sit down at the piano, or gather in brass ensembles, the "portable orchestra" of the guitar was perfectly suited to the itinerant country player. It could be rhythmic or melodic, punctuate the lyrics or fill them out, and it slung over the shoulder more comfortably than a barrelhouse piano.

Slowly, in the years following the Civil War, the music became identifiable and more formalized, although it was still not referred to as "the

Above: In the early 1920s, Paramount, Okeh, and Columbia were the three leading companies to issue what became known as "race" records, a generic term for records aimed at the black consumer. It was coined by Okeh's highly capable recording director, Ralph Peer, who began the label's "race" series.

Right: Alberta Hunter, pictured here in the early 1930s, is reputed to have run away to Chicago at the age of eleven to begin a distinguished career that would span seven decades. She was a blues-based cabaret singer who did much to bring early "classic" blues into the popular mainstream. From 1956 until 1977 she combined music with a nursing career at a New York hospital and continued performing into old age. She died in 1984.

blues". The color blue had been associated with melancholy for centuries, and so "blue feelings", shortened to "the blues", would have been a familiar term, but as yet no singer specialized in this unformed music; indeed, even entertainers of the 1920s and '30s frequently included other folk and popular tunes in their repertoires as they saw fit. As late as the 1950s, singers such as Big Bill Broonzy and Josh White actually moved away from hard core blues on the assumption that white audiences wanted folksy tales of railroad men, sharecroppers and city dandies; of John Henry and Stack O' Lee.

Nevertheless, something we would recognize as the blues became established in the first two decades of the twentieth century, in time to feed the burgeoning record industry, and verbal evidence suggests that it developed from existing lively dance forms, jigs and reels, before acquiring an additional voice: slow and introspective.

By 1902 Ma Rainey, a sometime performer with the traveling Rabbit Foot Minstrels, was including blues in her minstrel shows, and others followed. It may be that most of the early blues stars on record were women in city clothes because blacks were consciously choosing to dignify their music, to incorporate it into mainstream vaudeville, an "equal opportunity" industry based on urban theaters.

Furthermore, the blues was being tailored, as were the earlier "coon songs", ragtime, and jazz itself, to appeal to the majority white audience with money to spend who were looking for a little cultural novelty from the wrong side of the tracks. This curiosity had a long history: the nineteenth-century "nigger minstrel" bands were often white performers in "black face", while in 1929 the first talking pictures featured a white Jew, Al Jolson, as *The Jazz Singer*. British readers who are too young to remember Jolson may however recall how, until the 1970s, Saturday night television was blighted by the determinedly jolly *Black and White Minstrel Show*, an entertainment that would now understandably be rejected as racist, but at the time was merely the last gasp of a traditional form of theater as politically innocent as the golliwog on a jar of strawberry jelly.

Another reason why the early years of blues recording were dominated by what are sometimes known as "classic" blues could have simply been a miscalculation on the part of the record companies who made two assumptions: firstly, that there was no worthwhile market among blacks for records, and secondly, that white record-buyers would rather hear the city women than the rural men. Since we are dependent on records for our understanding of the blues' development, this does of course mean that the picture is to a certain extent incomplete. However, the mail-order companies and their easy-payment schemes quickly democratized gramophone ownership, while records were cheaply pressed and sold from the backs of cars.

Before records, after the "nigger minstrels", came sheet music. This effectively formalized the blues for the first time into its typical twelve-bar, three-chord structure (though eight-bar blues also developed). The first lyric line is usually repeated – originally, perhaps, to give the singer a little breathing space to improvize a pay-off line for the verse – although such formality would have been largely foreign to the earlier "hollers", and the artist who has proved the longest-lived and most celebrated of all the great blues singers, John Lee Hooker, has never had much truck with it. All the same, the publication of sheet-music clearly played a vital role in shaping the blues as we now recognize it.

In 1920 Mamie Smith made her first record for the Okeh label in New York, "That Thing Called Love". Its success led to her second recording, "Crazy Blues", on which she was backed by her Jazz Hounds, and it was the huge sales of this disc that confirmed there was a market for blues records. It also established Smith as a star, and she toured the theater circuit for the rest of her career, before dying in Harlem in 1946.

The floodgates were opened following "Crazy Blues", and numerous record companies entered the market. They may have been a little slow to appreciate the level of appeal among black audiences, but in the meantime the field became accessible to the many women performers who had been seasoned by their years in the minstrel shows and vaudeville. This meant that a female perspective was possible, in both writing and singing, to a degree that has rarely been equaled since – "man with guitar" is still, after all, the abiding image of rock music as it was to become with the blues.

An outstanding example of blues from the "classic" era was 'Downhearted Blues', written and first recorded by Alberta Hunter and a huge hit in a 1923 cover version by Bessie Smith, of whom more later. Hunter was born in Memphis in 1895 and grew up in Chicago, first recording in 1921, in the wake of Mamie Smith's success, for the new Black Swan label. Chicago, which was soon to earn notoriety for its racketeering in the Prohibition era, was now taking over from New Orleans as the hub of the jazz world. Lucille Hegamin, born in Macon, Georgia, in 1897, and the pianist Lil Hardin, who played in King Oliver's Creole Jazz Band, were among the other blues women attracted by the city's musical life.

So too was Ida Cox, who was sometimes billed as "The Sepia Mae West". Also from Georgia, where she was born in 1896, Cox worked as a child in the White & Clark Black & Tan Minstrels and later with the Rabbit Foot troupe. Around 1920 she was performing in Atlanta with Jelly Roll Morton, the great New Orleans pianist, while in Chicago she had a celebrated partnership at the Plantation Club with King Oliver's band. (After Buddy Bolden, Oliver had been New Orleans's second great jazz-band leader.) This was the exalted company with whom Cox worked and toured successfully throughout the 1930s. Less active in her later years, though she recorded with Coleman Hawkins in 1961, Cox died in Knoxville, Tennessee, in 1967.

Ten years younger than Cox, and resisting the lure of Chicago, Victoria Spivey was one of the most powerful female singers of the era. In her teens she sang and played piano in and around her home town of Houston, Texas, sometimes working with the rural entertainer Blind Lemon Jefferson, before moving to St Louis, Missouri, in 1926 and recording her first hit, 'Black Snake Blues'. Unlike most of her rivals Spivey did not need to depend on a band,

although, like Cox, she recorded with Oliver and others, including Armstrong and the guitarist Lonnie Johnson. She preferred, however, to tour as a solo act, and survived to enjoy a second wave of fame during the European blues revival of the 1960s, by which time she was also owner of her own Spivey record label. There is a celebrated 1961 photograph of her posing with the young Bob Dylan, whose early repertoire was steeped in the blues. Spivey continued to work until shortly before her death in 1976.

Beulah "Sippie" Wallace, born in 1898 and also from Houston, was another graduate of the touring tent shows, before moving to Chicago in 1923 at the start of the recording boom. One of her earliest recordings, 'Mail Train Blues', featured the ubiquitous Louis Armstrong on cornet, and he appears on a number of her 1920's records. Wallace left show-business in 1929 to be organist at the Leland Baptist Church in Detroit, later becoming director of the National Convention of Gospel Choirs and Choruses in Chicago. Apart from brief come-backs, such as a 1945 recording with boogie pianist Albert Ammons, Wallace remained out of the public eye until being rediscovered in the 1960s. In the 1970s she recorded with Bonnie Raitt, with whom she was reunited in 1982, four years before her death, to cut an album for Atlantic as the last of the "classic" blues women.

Other female singers who came to prominence in the 1920s, the first decade of the commercial record industry, included Clara Smith from South Carolina, Trixie Smith from Atlanta (clearly the surname Smith was a help to aspiring blues chanteuses born in the 1890s) and Kansas City's Julia Lee. Lee's career was largely confined to her native city, where she worked as a pianist in her brother George's band in the 1920s. The lively recordings on which her unjustly limited reputation largely rests – some cut with Jay McShann's band – came in the 1940s, and the usual topic of her distinctive rhythm and blues style is hinted at by song titles such as 'Snatch and Grab It', 'I Didn't Like It the First Time', 'My Man Stands Out', and 'All This Beef and Big Ripe Tomatoes'.

This strain of the blues – nurtured in the tent

shows and moving into the clubs and vaudeville theatres – was an element of citified jazz which spread out from New Orleans and traveled north up the Mississippi to Memphis and St Louis, west to Kansas City and east to Chicago. As we have seen, it was the style that first attracted the attention of the record industry. The most potent

line of the blues, however, was growing and growling in the Mississippi Delta, and after paying our respects to the first of the "classic" blues singers, Ma Rainey, and the greatest of them all, Bessie Smith, we travel from Texas, across to the southeast and then to the Delta, where the rural blues was taking root.

Above: Sippie Wallace enjoyed a comeback in the 1960s when, like Victoria Spivey, she became a star attraction at the blues festivals that were now playing to mainly white audiences.

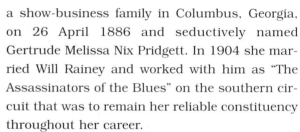

ma rainey

Ma Rainey (who preferred to be dignified by the title "Madame") took the blues on a journey from the traveling tent shows of the early years of the century to the southern vaudeville of the 1920s. Known as the "mother of the blues" and one of the decade's first female stars, she was born into a show-business family in Columbus, Georgia, on 26 April 1886 and seductively named Gertrude Melissa Nix Pridgett. In 1904 she married Will Rainey and worked with him as "The Assassinators of the Blues" on the southern circuit that was to remain her reliable constituency throughout her career.

She kept her husband's name after their brief marriage, and later joined a number of touring troupes including the celebrated Rabbit Foot Minstrels. After this apprenticeship she formed her own Georgia Jazz Band, an evening-dress outfit of brass and percussion led by pianist Georgia Tom. Ma, a short, stocky and plain-featured woman, made her entrance from a giant gramophone, bedecked with jewels and feathers, singing in a deep and often lascivious voice, and making up with showmanship what she lacked in physical beauty.

Signed to Paramount, she cut some hundred songs during her 1923–9 heyday, a substantial catalogue for the time. Those influenced by her included Bessie Smith, but for the most part her disciples adopted a more "citified" approach to the music. Rainey, meanwhile, retained country roots in the sound of the guitarist Tampa Red, a member of her band, and in recordings with such rural stars as Blind Blake.

The Depression, heralded by the stock market crash of 1929, was a blow to such artists, as was the advent of the popular cinema. Rainey retired in 1933 and invested her remaining savings. She died of a heart attack back home in Georgia on 22 December 1939.

Far left: Ma Rainey, pictured in the early 1920s. While her blues were more homespun than some of her more sophisticated contemporaries, Ma Rainey's lavish wardrobe made her look every inch the "classic" blues queen that she was.

Left: Ma Rainey with an unknown admirer early in her career.

screamin' and hollerin'

"There's one kind favor I ask of you
Please see that my grave is kept clean"

From 'See That My Grave Is Kept Clean' by Blind Lemon Jefferson

On 15 May 1929, at the age of thirty-five, Bessie Smith went into a New York recording studio as she had often done during the past six years. With the American economy crashing through the floor, the choice of song was fitting: 'Nobody Knows You When You're Down and Out'. She was backed on this occasion by Ed Allen on cornet, Garvin Bushell and Greely Walton on saxophones and Cyrus St Clair on tuba. She was also reunited with the pianist from her early recordings, Clarence Williams. The voice is less pure than it had been six years earlier, but the tinge of coarseness imparted by hard living and hard drinking adds even greater power – a weight of weary experience – to her marvelous delivery. It is just one stunning example of her mature style, but enough to demonstrate why her influence continues to reverberate, why the "Empress of the Blues" still exerts a power over listeners and would-be blues artists alike. Ironically, her recording career was soon to falter and then, too early, to fade away.

The era of the "classic" blues singer exactly spanned the period between Mamie Smith's first hit in 1920 and the early 1930s, when the ravages of the Depression curtailed so many promising careers. During this fertile epoch for women performers, Bessie Smith towered above the others in commercial appeal and range of expression; and while, today, the others may sound somewhat quaint, the Empress still reigns.

Left: The system of sharecropping operated on the largely false premise that planters would make advances to tenants in return for half the proceeds of the crop. In reality, planters manipulated their accounts so that tenants were kept in permanent debt.

Above: A clapboard house in a Chicago slum neighborhood in 1941. For over half a century, overcrowding (quite often several families would occupy one room on a shift basis) and poor sanitation made Chicago's tenement slums both dangerous and disease-ridden.

From busking as a teenager, Smith graduated, in 1912, to working locally with Ma Rainey, the first of several meetings between the two women who were to become the biggest blues stars of the 1920s. Throughout the decade she made hundreds of recordings, but sadly her career was one of the many that fell victim to the Depression, and after 1931 she only recorded once more, in 1933. This time the band included Jack Teagarden on trombone, Chu Berry on tenor sax, and Benny Goodman on clarinet; and the power on such songs as 'Do Your Duty' and 'Gimme a Pig Foot' is undimmed. All the same the session failed to revive her career; it is significant that her flat fee for the recording was fifty dollars per side, just a quarter of the money

she was commanding a decade earlier. America was beginning to find its feet again, but Smith's day was gone.

For the last four years of her life she continued to work in theatrical revue, however, both on tour and in city residencies, until tragically, while traveling between dates with the Broadway Rastus Revue, she was involved in a car crash in Coahoma, Mississippi, and died in a Clarksdale hospital on 26 September 1937. Racial motives were at one time ascribed to an alleged delay in transporting her there, but this story has subsequently been refuted. (Her injuries were such that she would probably have died had she crashed in the hospital yard: one of her arms was amputated, but loss of blood and shock had already condemned her.) With her death the "classic" blues era, mortally wounded by the Depression, was also gone. Its greatest exponent had not been invited to record even once during the previous four years.

It was not until 1970 that Bessie Smith's grave was properly marked, and this symbolic act heralded renewed appreciation for her genius, prompted in part by a grateful and enthusiastic Janis Joplin. In 1971 Smith's complete recordings, repackaged, were awarded the *Grand Prix du Disque* at the Montreux Jazz Festival, since when her reputation has been secure.

The 1920s did not, of course, belong entirely to the "classic" blues – the jazz-band blues of the cities – and by the middle of the decade the record companies were belatedly waking up to the "rootsier" appeal of the country blues. The First World War had stimulated migration from the countryside to the industrial cities of the North and the major ports, where industries like steel and ship-building were busy supplying the war effort. This, however, simply accelerated a drift that had been in motion at least since the turn of the century. The proportion of the population in the South who were black had been steadily declining anyway, with the exception of the fertile alluvial land enclosed within the Mississippi Delta.

These new industrial workers had money to spend on "their" music – the country blues they had left behind as well as the citified version – prompting the increased production of what came to be designated "race records". The country blues were developing on three main fronts: Texas and Louisiana; the East Coast from Florida northwards; and, above all, the Mississippi Delta.

One of the biggest companies to feed this growing demand was the Chicago-based Paramount Records. Historically purveyors of furniture and furnishings, by the start of the First World War the company was selling gramophones, from which producing records was a logical progression. These they pressed using cheap materials, enabling them to set prices which undercut their rivals. As their success

grew they were able to buy out some labels and distribute others, thereby increasing their hold on the market until, like so many companies, they were brought down in the Depression.

Early successes with the homespun music of singer and banjo-player Papa Charlie Jackson led Paramount to sign more significant rural talents like Blind Lemon Jefferson and Blind Blake, who were advertised alongside well-known stars such as Ma Rainey and Ida Cox. A 1924 advertisement for a Jackson record published in the black newspaper *Chicago Defender* confirms that until this time it was the women who held sway. "Be convinced," it said, "that this man Charlie can sing and play the Blues even better than a woman can." Clearly, such a revolutionary concept needed hammering home. This was a period when the idea of the specialist blues singer – as a development from the "songster" who would incorporate all manner of popular song styles into his entertainment – was only beginning to be established.

During his brief recording career Blind Lemon Jefferson brought a totally new intensity,

Below: Bessie Smith was born in Chattanooga, Tennessee, on 15 April 1894 and was orphaned by the time she was eight. After a long touring apprenticeship she was first recorded in 1923 (despite having been told by several talent scouts that her voice was too "rough" to record). The resulting single, 'Downhearted Blues', sold 750,000 copies in a year, making her the most celebrated female blues singer of the 1920s. She won the hearts of her black audiences as much for her uncompromising lyrics as for her passionate delivery. Her more erotic songs spoke of the potency of black men over "brown-skinned ones", which naturally delighted her black audiences.

complexity and technical ingenuity to the rural blues. His voice was high and lonesome, his guitar alternating rhythmic surges with single-note runs, and he was always willing to sacrifice strict tempo and verse structure to follow the feeling. Lightnin' Hopkins was one of the younger bluesmen who acted as his guide for a while, and undoubtedly learned from him, while Jefferson's influence on white music is indicated by the fact that rockabilly pioneer Carl Perkins revived his 'Match Box Blues', and Bob Dylan repeated Blind Lemon's request that his "grave be kept clean", in a version of the song that is a respectful pastiche of Jefferson's erratic but potent style.

A link between the field hollers and work songs of earlier days and the blues of Jefferson is provided by two older performers who were nonetheless influenced in their turn by the younger man. Huddie Ledbetter, known as Leadbelly, was an important exponent of the old songster tradition (he is discussed in greater detail in the next chapter), as was Lightnin' Hopkins's cousin, born in Leona, Texas, around 1880, who usually worked under the name Texas Alexander.

By the late 1920s black America's musical and migratory paths were beginning to spread. When Alexander went to New York in 1927 to record for the Okeh label, his passionate, musically undisciplined vocals were given some shape by the melodic guitar lines of Lonnie Johnson, while in the same year the versatile Johnson, one of the most sophisticated and inventive guitarists of the era, contributed his guitar solos to some of the finest records by Louis Armstrong's Hot Five, a far cry from Alexander's work songs.

Johnson was born in New Orleans, probably on 8 February 1889, although some sources make him five years younger. This was Buddy Bolden's era, and while the "Crescent City" was undoubtedly the cradle of jazz, it is less renowned for its solo blues performers. Johnson, however, made a living in its red-light district from about 1910 before beginning the life of the traveling musician. He even visited England with a musical revue in 1917, and back home worked on riverboats as well as on the TOBA (Theater Owners' Booking Agency) circuit in the South. His recording career began when he won a St Louis talent contest in 1925 which led to a contract with Okeh.

By the end of the decade Johnson was a star, and from 1928 onward he recorded a series of guitar duets with Eddie Lang, a jazzman and a pioneer of the plectrum technique employed to give extra bite to solo lines and crispness to rhythm work. Lang had also worked with Joe Venuti, Tommy Dorsey, Red Nichols, and Bix Beiderbecke, among many others, as well as recording several guitar arrangements of classical pieces. When "slumming it" as a blues player he used the pseudonym Blind Willie Dunn, but

Below: Blind Lemon Jefferson was born in 1897 in Couchman, Texas. Blind from birth, or partially so (this publicity picture shows him wearing glasses) he was unable to work on his father's dirt farm, and so learned to play the guitar. He cut his first record in Chicago in 1925 and died in that city, lying frozen in a gutter in the pre-Christmas snow of 1929. The exact cause of this death remains a mystery.

Cordially Yours Blind Lemon Jefferson

the combination of his technical prowess and Johnson's more forthright style make their guitar collaborations some of the greatest in the history of jazz.

Johnson also toured with Bessie Smith throughout the South and returned to New York to appear on his own radio show, but, like Smith, he found that fame was not Depression-proof, and during the early 1930s he was forced to take various manual jobs. After making a comeback in 1937 Johnson's career proceeded in fits and starts, including a European tour in 1963 as part of the American Folk Blues Festival, and he died in Toronto in 1970. His clean, crisp approach to a melodic guitar line was to prove as influential as the electric pioneering of T-Bone Walker, and today it lives on in the solos of B.B.King.

The last of the pioneer bluesmen from this southern swathe across Texas and Louisiana to demand a mention is Mance Lipscomb, who was born in Navasota, Texas, on 9 April 1895. He is of particular interest because he spent most of his life as a farmer, playing only at local dances, until he was discovered by folk-musicologist Chris Strachwitz in 1960 and recorded for his Arhoolie label. This meant that later generations of blues enthusiasts could hear the early rural blues, ballads and hymns of Texas performed by an engaging and still-sprightly artist uncolored by later developments in the music. Between 1960 and 1973, three years before his death, Lipscomb recorded, toured, and took part in a number of films and documentaries, his work combining to make an invaluable "living archive" of the blues. An almost exact parallel is found in the work of Mississippi John Hurt, who was born in 1893 but almost completely confined to entertaining at local dances until brought into the limelight by folk fan Tom Hoskins in 1963.

Another strand of the blues thrived in the Southeast, from Florida up through Georgia and into the Carolinas. Blind Blake was born in Jacksonville, Florida, some time in the early 1890s, but soon moved north into Georgia where he worked as a street busker. His guitar style harked back to ragtime, deft, danceable and syncopated, and his local popularity attracted

Left: Charley Patton, who was unusually light-skinned with wavy hair, was born in 1887 in Edwards, Mississippi, and worked on Will Dockery's plantation as a child. In the 1920s he traveled with other pioneer Delta bluesmen like Tommy Johnson and Willie Brown before cutting his first records for Paramount in 1929. In his book *Blues Makers*, Samuel Charters describes Patton as "a small, intense, fretful man who blustered his way out of fights, sang with fierce strength, and survived as best he could in a violent countryside". He died of a heart condition on 28 April 1934 leaving a small but forceful catalog of recordings including 'Screamin' and Hollerin' the Blues', a title that encapsulates the raw power of the man.

the attention of record scout Mayo Williams, who recorded him in Chicago for Paramount from 1926. In the late 1920s he worked with Ma Rainey, Gus Cannon, Papa Charlie Jackson, and other musicians working in Chicago. However, while his nimble picking would be an influence on later stars such as Big Bill Broonzy and Josh White, his own star faded in the early 1930s and he died, back in Florida, in around 1933.

Blind Willie McTell enjoyed a longer career, still recording in the mid-1950s. Born in Thomson, Georgia, on 5 May 1901 and raised in Statesboro (the subject of his best-known song, 'Statesboro Blues'). McTell was a street singer, often found in the company of another blind artist, Willie Johnson. His high-pitched, plaintive voice was driven by the rhythm of a big twelve-string guitar which gave his recordings a distinctive, full sound. From the late 1920s he made records in Atlanta for various labels and in

Above: Skip James was one of the great blues stylists, a unique performer whose eerie, falsetto singing voice and minor-tuned guitar were unusually compelling.

1940 contributed a catalog of music to the project sponsored by the Library of Congress aimed at recording for posterity the folk music styles of America. In the 1920s Atlanta was a thriving blues town, centered on the red-light district of Decatur Street, where other briefly successful local artists included Peg-Leg Howell and Barbecue Bob. Like McTell, Bob played a twelve-string, fretting it with a bottleneck to produce a stinging, percussive sound.

Three hundred miles northeast of Atlanta in the Piedmont Hills of North Carolina, a leading exponent of what came to be identified as the "Piedmont" style of blues guitar was yet another partially-sighted guitarist, Blind Boy Fuller. Born in Wadesboro some time in 1908, he worked as a traveling musician in his twenties by which time he was completely blind. Fuller died in 1941, but his delicate, ragtime-inflected style is remembered through the prolific recordings he made for the American Record Company (ARC) in the latter half of the 1930s.

Meanwhile, one of those contemporaries he undoubtedly learned from survived long enough to be rediscovered and recorded in the 1960s and early '70s. Even though he could not be described as a pure blues musician, the Reverend Gary Davis – who was also blind – is surely the real master of the Carolina blues. Born on 30 April 1896 in Laurens, South Carolina, and completely self-taught, Davis combined music with Baptist preaching. He first recorded for ARC in 1935. Around 1944 his wife got a job as a cook in New York and he spent most of the rest of his life there until his death in 1972. In much of his work – even his celebrated pop song 'Candyman' and his double-entendre 'Hesitation Blues' – the syncopations of ragtime are never far away. Ragtime, like bluegrass, can be played with stunning technical brilliance and no feel whatsoever, but Davis was a virtuoso with soul.

This brief trawl of the Southeast is completed by the duo Tampa Red and Georgia Tom. Both were born in Georgia – Tom (Thomas A. Dorsey) on 1 July 1899 and Tampa Red maybe a year later – but it was in Chicago, in around 1928, that the two teamed up as a piano-guitar double act. They termed their sound "hokum", and it was a jaunty, harmonizing music, often with double entendre lyrics, as on their huge hit 'It's Tight Like That', which was swiftly covered by Lonnie Johnson. However, this mood was out of keeping with the Depression, and Dorsey turned instead to religious music, composing such gospel standards as 'Precious Lord' and 'That's Good News', while Tampa Red tended toward jazz with his group the Chicago Five.

Although the country blues – rural in style even if it headed toward Chicago in search of a

record contract – was largely a male province, there was one remarkable exception. Memphis Minnie was one of the most distinctive and inventive guitarists of the day. As a child in New Orleans she played for local parties before arriving in Memphis in her early teens. In 1930, performing with her first husband Kansas Joe McCoy, she moved to Chicago where the duo had a big hit with 'Bumble Bee'. In the mid-1930s, having been divorced, Minnie recorded with jazz line-ups for a while before forming another duo with her second husband, Little Son Joe (Ernest Lawlars). As in her previous marital partnership Minnie was the dominant one musically, a fact exemplified by hits such as 1941's 'Me and My Chauffeur', a double entendre blues, in which her deft, crisp lead guitar lines – unusual for the time – hint at the bent and sustained notes that would become a feature of electric blues.

As one might expect with an area as vast as Texas and Louisiana – from Dallas in the north to New Orleans in the southeast – there is no cohesive style of early blues to characterize the region. Any links between the field shouts of Texas Alexander and the post-war electric wizardry of T-Bone Walker, between the nimble jazz

Below: The handsome, vibrant figure of Memphis Minnie, who was born Lizzie Douglas in Algiers, New Orleans, on 3 June 1897, was "serenading" along Beale Street, Memphis, with her guitar by the time she was fifteen. Although she lived until 1973 she barely worked after the mid-1950s, but her influence could be heard in the work of artists such as Big Mama Thornton and the peerless British blues interpreter Jo-Ann Kelly.

Below: Lonnie Johnson was one of the first great "modern" blues guitarists. An inventive instrumentalist, his single string solos have been emulated by performers of both jazz and blues.

lines of Lonnie Johnson and the sly, warmly-delivered folk tales of Lightnin' Hopkins, are more geographical than musical. There may be more detectable similarities between the bluesmen of the Southeast – a lightness of touch, perhaps, a jaunty ragtime feel – but there are still too many exceptions to prove the rule. The blues

is above all a traveling music, receptive to anything it meets, adaptable, organic.

However, when we look to the Mississippi Delta we find a unique focus. It is said that "the Mississippi Delta begins in the lobby of the Peabody Hotel in Memphis and ends on Catfish Row in Vicksburg", and broadly speaking it is in

the farmland that lies between these metropolitan extremes that a common feeling for the blues seems to exist as nowhere else.

For all that, the great exponents of "Delta" blues are anything but clones: a record by Robert Johnson or Howlin' Wolf, Muddy Waters or John Lee Hooker has proclaimed its individuality by the first bar, and yet all these Delta bluesmen seem to be soul brothers. Their common identity comes partly from an urgency of rhythm, a tautness which drives the song forward, even when the chosen tempo is stately, coupled with an emotional intensity, a brooding, surly power, even a sense of fear: Johnson's notion of there being a hellhound on his trail typifies this feeling, while in other songs the "hellhound" may be a jealous husband, tuberculosis or a disastrous natural calamity, like the flood of 1927.

Even acknowledging the inevitable exceptions – the spidery guitar and falsetto voice of Skip James is an obvious example – why is it that, taken as a whole, the Delta blues has an unalloyed character not found elsewhere?

I suspect that the reason is similar to the one that finds the roots of hillbilly music in the Appalachian Mountains between Kentucky and the Carolinas. Although it is difficult to detect African rhythms in the blues, it is easy to hear Celtic strains in country and western. But migrants escaping starvation in Ireland and Scotland settled in many parts of America, so why do we identify their New World music with a particular region of the east?

Presumably it is because here the migrants found themselves in isolated, inward-looking farming and mining communities where their music could take root and find its own identity unsullied by outside influences. By the time improved communications and changing economic and social patterns opened up the mountains, hillbilly music was indelibly established.

In the same way, the fertile farmlands of the Delta represented another cultural backwater with severely limited horizons. Here, black workers could indeed find work, but virtually as slaves of the white landowners, and so perhaps it is this enforced isolation that gives the indige-

nous blues its focus and power.

Whatever musical ragbag Delta bluesman Charley Patton grew up with – an older musician called Henry Sloan, probably in the "songster" tradition, is cited as an influence – there are no ragtime rhythms, no New Orleans jazz, no Celtic reels or German polkas in his mature work. He may have been a musical all-rounder in his youth, but by the time he came to make records Patton had refined his style into a Mississippi moan: a threatening and desperate musing that often dissolved into wordless humming or so dislocated the lyric that the precise sense was lost, leaving only the dark mood.

Above: With progressively failing eyesight, Blind Willie McTell, pictured here in the late 1920s, spent much of his adolescence wandering the country playing music before finally going blind in his late teens. Thereafter, he gave up music for eight years until the popularity of the blues found him in the recording studio at the behest of Okeh's Ralph Peer. McTell continued to record well into his fifties.

PROFILE

robert johnson

If there has to be an archetypal image of a blues singer, it might as well be Robert Johnson: he lived in the Mississippi Delta, he was a performer of unusual inventiveness, his topics were sin and sex, he was reputed to have sold his soul to the devil in return for his musical talent, and he was dead at twenty-seven, allegedly poisoned by a jealous husband.

Johnson was probably born on 8 May 1911, in Hazlehurst, Mississippi, and was his mother's eleventh child, the result of an affair with a farm worker called Noah Johnson. He grew up on a plantation near Robinsonville, where he learned to play the harmonica, and in his late teens came to know local bluesmen who were playing at "Saturday night balls", like Son House. Johnson would also have become aware of Charley Patton, as well as other local stars like Willie Brown, Howlin' Wolf and Tommy Johnson. He was keen to play guitar, but Son House has attested to the fact that he had no talent for the instrument. At the age of twenty, having already been married and divorced, Johnson disappeared from Robinsonville for a year or more, during which time he married again. He reappeared at a dance where Son House and Willie Brown were playing and insisted on sitting in on guitar. His hamfistedness had completely disappeared. "And man! He was so good!" House recalled. "When he finished, all our mouths were standing open."

Thereafter, Johnson traveled widely, though he never settled down away from Mississippi. As with so many blues artists of the time he did not limit his repertoire and was willing to play anything anyone wanted to hear. He was aided in this by possessing an uncanny ability to repeat a song note for note having only heard it once before.

However, his place in history is secured by his remarkable catalogue of blues compositions, recorded in just two extended sessions in San Antonio (November 1936) and Dallas (June 1937). His urgent vocal delivery was in the Patton tradition, but unlike the older man Johnson had precise diction rather than an emotive moan or "holler".

Elmore James founded his career on Johnson's 'Dust My Broom', while 'Walking Blues' and 'Come On In My Kitchen' were in many a bluesman's repertoire. 'Crossroads' and 'Love in Vain' were revived by Cream and the Rolling Stones respectively, 'Hellhound On My Trail' and 'Stones In My Passway' are among the most chillingly confessional of all blues songs, and his 'Sweet Home Chicago' is one of the greatest of all blues standards.

Having learned from the Delta men of the early 1930s, Johnson passed the torch on to those, like Muddy Waters, who took the music north. So, as well as contributing his own unmatched talents to the blues, he represents a vital link in the chain which joins the Delta to the northern cities. On 16 August 1938, while performing at Greenwood, Mississippi, he apparently drank poisoned whiskey (or according to some testimony was stabbed) and died a few hours later.

Left: Robert Johnson, pictured here in the mid-1930s, did not make his first known recording until he was twenty-five. Although an adept mimic (on his recordings of Delta songs he often sounds like Son House) he pioneered a combination of passionate singing, powerful lyrics, and super-charged guitar-playing. It was from this that Muddy Waters and Elmore James would draw the inspiration to turn local Delta blues into the rhythm and blues of the post-war era.

the blues moves north

"I'm so poor, baby, I have to lean up against the fence to gargle
Yeah, now baby, well I believe I'll change towns
Yeah, I'm down so low baby, ooo lord, yeah, I declare I'm looking up at down"

From 'Looking Up At Down' by Big Bill Broonzy

The first news of the Wall Street Crash on 24 October 1929 probably caused few ripples among the sharecroppers and plantation workers of the South, but before long the entire country was overwhelmed by the most profound economic disaster ever to be experienced by a first world country. An industrial society moving more and more toward a mass production-based economy clearly depends on an equivalent mass of customers for its output, and in the 1920s the ballooning growth of American industry, ushered in by Henry Ford's development of conveyor-belt car production, moved steadily ahead of consumers' ability to support it.

Finally, on what came to be known as Black Thursday, a catastrophic lack of confidence among investors led to panic on the New York Stock Exchange causing the paper value of shares to collapse by billions of dollars. In the weeks that followed banks went out of business, loans and mortgages were called in, factories closed, their suppliers went bankrupt, workers were laid off. Almost half the population hovered on either side of a basic subsistence level, and at the very bottom of the social pyramid rural blacks faced starvation. The drift from the land in the South which had been gathering pace since the beginning of the century – more than a million moved from farms into

Left: Between 1910 and 1930, nearly two million poor blacks left the southern states bound for the big cities of the North in what was to be the biggest migration in American history.

33

Right: Rice Miller (Sonny Boy II) was one of the first blues radio stars. His regular slot on KFFA radio (King Biscuit Time) was sponsored by a flour mill owner, who used the singer's sobriquet to sell his products.

Below: Harmonica player extraordinaire Sonny Boy Williamson I was a Chicago star before his death in 1948.

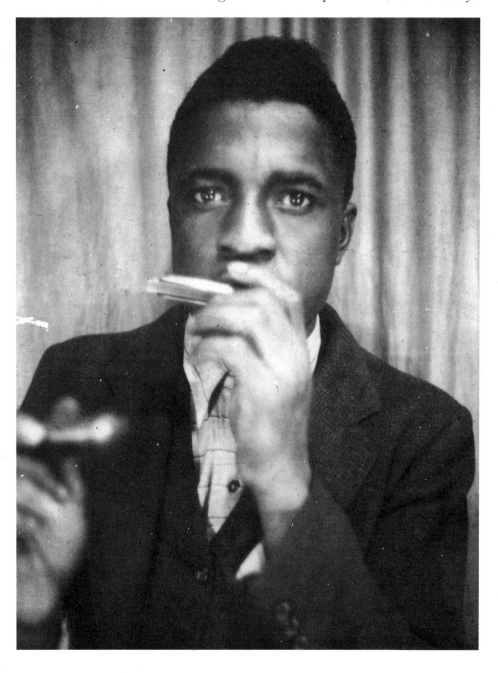

urban ghettoes during the 1920s – now became one of desperation.

However, not all of the Delta men made the move north at this time. Robert Johnson stayed at home, as did his mentor Son House. Born on 21 March 1902 on a plantation near Clarksdale, House and his family moved around the South in search of work. From the late 1920s until the early 1940s he was a popular entertainer at local parties and dances although he never committed himself to music full-time. In many ways he was the archetypal Delta blues singer – technically straightforward but passionate, as if always

fighting to contain his anguish and corral it into musical form – but, in spite of his towering talent, he was largely lost to music until the 1960s, when he was rediscovered living in New York and became a hero of the festival circuit. Ill-health curtailed his new career in the early 1970s and he died in 1988.

Even more influential on local bluesmen was Tommy Johnson, who was born in Mississippi in the mid-1890s. In his youth Johnson found jobs where he could, as well as working as an itinerant musician, encountering Charley Patton and Willie Brown on his travels. He first recorded in 1928 and later in life was usually based in Jackson, Mississippi. Among his first records was 'Cool Water Blues', based on a traditional song and beginning with the celebrated line: "I asked for water, and she gave me gasoline". Howlin' Wolf, one of those who undoubtedly learned from Johnson, appropriated the song in the 1950s as well as aspects of Johnson's showmanship, which included throwing the guitar over his head and playing it behind his neck – a trick imitated subsequently by later artists such as T-Bone Walker and Jimi Hendrix. Johnson died of a heart attack playing at a house party in 1956. Had he survived a little longer into the period of the blues revival his key part in the blues story would be more widely recognized.

These artists learned from another undeservedly obscure talent who has been referred to several times already, Willie Brown. He was born in Clarksdale on 6 August 1900, and from his teens traveled the southern circuit before moving to New York with Son House in the early 1940s in search of work outside music. Although he might sound a little crude today, Brown's gruff vocal delivery and forceful guitar playing left a distinct mark on his contemporaries. He died of a heart attack in 1952.

This was a year before Howlin' Wolf finally took the risk and made it to Chicago to join Muddy Waters. Meanwhile, the Tennessee harmonica player John Lee "Sonny Boy" Williamson, sometimes known as Sonny Boy Williamson I, made the journey to Chicago much earlier, in 1934, when the Depression had reached its lowest depths. Born on 30 March 1914, he died tragically young on 1 June 1948, his skull fractured by a mugger outside Chicago's Plantation Club. As with Tommy Johnson, his early death made him a shadowy figure to the new blues audience that developed in the early 1960s, and his profile was further obscured by the hi-jacking of his name by Rice Miller, ironically a much older man but now identified as Sonny Boy Williamson II.

John Lee worked as a hobo musician around Tennessee, including Memphis and across into Arkansas, before making the journey north. He first recorded for Bluebird in 1937, and, as the first harmonica player to reveal the virtuoso potential of the humble mouth organ, his importance in the modern era of Chicago blues can not be over-emphasized. The attractions of this

instrument to bluesmen were obvious: it was cheap, portable and could be used in conjunction with a guitar as the basis of a one-man band. From Leadbelly to Bob Dylan, artists have used it as a musical punctuation mark, stabbing and wheezing its way between the lyric lines, but John Lee Williamson moved it into the spotlight, opening the way for younger men such as Little Walter to raise its status to that of a jazz-blues solo instrument.

The 1950s was to prove not just the golden age of Chicago blues but one in which the harmonica would begin to play an increasingly vital role, becoming an essential component of the standard group line-up. With his decade of club work in the city and exceptional records, such as 'Good Morning Little Schoolgirl' and 'Early in the Morning', the "first" Sonny Boy Williamson was

Above: Josh White was born and raised in South Carolina but is best remembered as a New York singer and guitarist. He specialized in blues of the Piedmont variety and was especially popular among the American white folk-blues audiences.

Right: Lightnin' Hopkins was one of the best-known bluesmen of the 1930s and '40s. However, in the mid-1950s, perhaps due to the rock 'n' roll revolution, recording opportunities dried up until he was rediscovered by blues historian and producer, Sam Charters, in 1959. For the remainder of his career, though still often reluctant to leave Houston, Hopkins enjoyed greater celebrity than ever on the folk club and festival circuits, and in 1968 blues film-maker, Les Blank, shot a celebration of his life, *The Blues Accordin' to Lighnin' Hopkins*. He died in 1982.

an encouragement not just to his namesake and Little Walter but to Billy Boy Arnold, Walter Horton, Snooky Pryor and a whole generation of blues harmonica players.

Rice Miller, on the other hand, lived long enough to experience both the earliest days of blues recording and 1960s guest appearances with British enthusiasts like the Yardbirds. Born in Glendora, Mississippi, on 5 December 1899 he became a child entertainer and served the familiar apprenticeship as an itinerant musician throughout the South, initially billing himself as Little Boy Blue. Erstwhile musical partners included Sunnyland Slim, Howlin' Wolf, Robert Johnson, Elmore James and Robert Lockwood Jr. In the mid-1930s he even appeared at the home of white country music, Nashville's Grand Ol' Opry, where one of the first resident musicians had been another black harmonica player, DeFord Bailey.

Local commercial radio grew apace in the 1930s – concerts at the Grand Ol' Opry were broadcast every week – and blues musicians as well as hillbilly artists began to be hired to pro-

vide live music for sponsored shows. It was when Rice Miller was hired with Lockwood to star in King Biscuit Time, transmitted on KFFA Radio from Helena, Arkansas, and networked into Mississippi, that he adopted the name Sonny Boy Williamson. (Presumably he knew that the original was by now in Chicago, beyond the radio station's range, although throughout his life he insisted that he took the name first.) He later capitalized on his radio fame by taking a band on the road as the King Biscuit Entertainers.

By the time Williamson arrived in Chicago in 1955, a middle-aged man, his harmonica style was mature and highly individual. He preferred playing a tiny instrument that he could cup in the palm of his hand, enabling him to confide in the microphone's ear rather than shriek at it, and, against an irresistible shuffle rhythm, was able to coax from the instrument a marvelous range of textures: pleading, threatening, boasting, punctuating or echoing his sly, breathy lyrics, spiralling into tiny fragments of delicate melody, or snarling at the bottom of the register.

On Williamson's first recording session for

the Chess label in Chicago he was provided with Muddy Waters' band – the best in town – and with it produced his first and biggest hit, 'Don't Start Me Talkin'. He had already recorded extensively for Trumpet in Jackson, Mississippi, but on Chess he began to compile a stunning catalog of blues classics. In 1963, toward the end of his life, Williamson had another huge hit with 'Help Me', which borrowed the riff that had helped Memphis band Booker-T and the MGs to success with their classic soul instrumental 'Green Onions'. Other sides, such as 'Fattening Frogs for Snakes', 'Your Funeral and My Trial', 'Nine Below Zero', and 'Bye Bye Bird', cut during Williamson's eight years on Chess, were equally strong.

He first came to Europe in 1963 with the American Folk Blues Festival, and soon afterward toured England with the Chris Barber Band and recorded with the Yardbirds. Between then and his death in 1965 he was often in England, a rakish, sly, and somewhat disreputable father figure to the blues bands that were flourishing in pub ballrooms and basement clubs up and down the country.

To return to our starting point in the 1930s, when Big Bill Broonzy was king of Chicago blues and emigration from the poverty-stricken South was gathering pace, one of the greatest of all the country blues singers was hustling a living on the streets of Houston, Texas. Sam "Lightnin'" Hopkins, born north of Houston in Centerville on 15 March 1912, was also one of the most prolifically recorded of all bluesmen despite never

Left: Roosevelt Sykes, born in Elmar, Arkansas, on 31 January 1906, was a graduate of the barrelhouse circuit. He was known as "The Honeydripper", although accounts vary as to whether he earned this sobriquet thanks to his sweet touch with the ladies or with the keyboard. In the late 1920s he was in St Louis working with Lonnie Johnson's wife Mary, among others, and in the 1930s was based in Chicago. Eventually, he moved back south to New Orleans where he died in 1983. However, he had survived long enough to find new fame as a festival performer, and in the meantime had formed a vital bridge between the itinerant, rural, southern blues of the 1920s and '30s and the electric blues of the post-war period.

making the great trek north.

In the early 1920s, still not in his teens, Hopkins left school to become a hobo musician, acting for a while as Blind Lemon Jefferson's guide – a 1959 track is called 'Reminiscences of Blind Lemon'. Around 1927 he teamed up with Texas Alexander as an itinerant duo, a relationship that lasted on and off into the 1950s. It was not until 1946, however, when the Aladdin label in Los Angeles teamed him with pianist "Thunder" Smith for a handful of records, that Hopkins acquired the nickname that would stick with him for the rest of his life. These were Lightnin' Hopkins' first recordings, but by 1947

Below: Leadbelly, pictured here in the early 1940s, was born Huddie Ledbetter in 1888. As a compelling bluesman he did much to convert mainstream white America to black music.

he was back in Houston recording for Gold Band as a solo artist.

Hopkins had a warm, expressive and confidential voice, sometimes humorous and racy, sometimes pleading for his woman to "take pity on po' Lightnin'". When playing up-tempo, whether on acoustic or heavily amplified guitar, he had one of the most infectious of all boogie rhythms, while his slow songs were decorated by delicate, swirling little guitar fills. To the familiar blues subject matter of hard times, whether economic or sexual, Hopkins added vignettes of country life (largely recollected from his home amid the urban motorway sprawl of Houston), and songs based on real-life events like 'Happy Blues for John Glenn' (the astronaut) and 'Hurricane Betsy'.

Throughout his long career Hopkins mixed long-standing relationships with record labels with a willingness to turn out cash-in-hand sessions, which partly explains his extraordinary productivity. Only genius, however, can account for the consistently high standards he achieved.

Although it has been noted that a guitar was the obvious choice of instrument for an itinerant southern bluesman, there was another circuit that could support the traveling piano-player. Outside the cities, serving the logging camps, farming communities, turpentine factories and railroad shanties, were barrelhouse bars, gambling houses and brothels where the extra volume obtained by pounding the keys had a clear advantage over guitar-picking. The pianist entertainers who worked in these places were usually not specialist bluesmen as such, but entertainers who could move from boogie-woogie to ballad as required.

"Little Brother" Montgomery, born on 18 April 1906 in Kentwood, Louisiana, was one such whose jazz-blues style was usually tagged "barrelhouse" after the boisterous venues – the bar often no more than a plank of wood supported by two barrels – in which this hybrid took root. During the 1920s he would regularly team up with guitarist Big Joe Williams to travel the southern circuit. By 1928, however, though he continued to work and record extensively in the South, he had made the move to Chicago where

he became a formative influence on the post-war generation of Chicago keyboard players like Otis Spann. In the mid-1950s Montgomery recorded with one of the younger breed of Chicago guitarists, Otis Rush, and in 1960 he made a record in London with Ken Colyer and Alexis Korner. From this time on Montgomery was able to add the festival circuit, often in Europe, to his itinerary. He died in Chicago in 1985.

Huddie Ledbetter, Leadbelly, only just lived into the electric era – he died in New York in 1949 – but in any case it is unlikely that he would have had much truck with Gibson guitars and amplifier stacks. Leadbelly looked back to the world of field hollers, plantation and chain-gang songs, keeping alive this vital link with the music's past, taking it from the post-slavery dirt farms and plantations to the concert halls of New York and even Paris.

It is doubtful whether this could have happened without the help of folklorists John Lomax and his son Alan. The elder Lomax began "collecting" American songs as a child, before going on to research extensively into the British song tradition. Later, the development of the cylinder recording method, whereby a vocalist sang into a funnel and their voice was translated through a membrane into grooves cut directly into a revolving wax cylinder, enabled him to expand his activities, and he published *Cowboy Songs and Other Frontier Ballads* in 1910. Eventually, in 1933, the Library of Congress commissioned him to build an archive of indigenous folk songs for posterity, and with the help of his teenage son John, Lomax began to assemble a vast catalog of recorded music. Among those preserved on Bakelite for the first time were Bukka White, recorded on Parchman Farm in 1940, Muddy Waters, recorded a year later on Stovall Plantation, and Leadbelly.

This Louisiana-born, Texas-raised entertainer began mixing performing with manual labour as a youth, and in 1912 was acting as Blind Lemon Jefferson's "eyes". Around 1916, however, he was jailed for assault. He later escaped, only to be re-imprisoned, this time for murder. In 1925 he was pardoned, but five years later received a ten-year sentence for assault with intent to murder. It was during this prison term in Angola State Penitentiary in Louisiana that he was first recorded by the Lomaxes, and it seems likely that it was thanks to their patronage that he was able to "sing his way out of prison" in 1934. Leadbelly remained under their wing for some time, employed as their chauffeur and promoted by them as a performer.

Another prison sentence for assault in 1939 confirmed that this barrel-chested man was destined to be a victim of his temperament, although between bouts of violence he established a nationwide reputation as one of the living repositories of the nation's folk culture, along with fellow artists such as white political songwriter Woody Guthrie and blues duo Sonny Terry and Brownie McGhee.

Leadbelly supported his deep-voiced, passionate singing with twelve-string guitar playing that made up in rhythmic drive what it lacked in technical subtlety. His catalog, either as writer or "reclaimer" from distant folk memory, included 'Rock Island Line', 'Midnight Special', 'Ella Speed' and 'Goodnight Irene'. Shortly after his death the

latter song was a hit for the Weavers, a white folk group which included Pete Seeger, and a few years later the British jazz-blues performer Lonnie Donegan based his act on Leadbelly's music and took 'Rock Island Line' to the top of the charts. These early glimmers of the 'blues revival' were enough to ensure the place of this ill-tempered convict in the hearts of a new generation of blues enthusiasts.

Another bridge between 1930s folk-blues and the 1960s was built by harmonica player Sonny Terry and guitarist Brownie McGhee, two top-class solo performers, but who are best remembered as one of the longest lasting partnerships in the blues. Although both widely traveled, their style is perhaps best seen as part of the Piedmont school. Terry (Saunders Terrell) was born on 24 October 1911 in Greensboro, North Carolina, the son of a harmonica player who performed "buckdances, reels and jigs", he has recalled, at local parties. At eleven he was injured in one eye, and five years later the other eye was also damaged, leaving him almost blind. He became a musical hobo, and by the mid-1930s had teamed up with Blind Boy Fuller. These two recorded together in New York where Terry also appeared in the Spirituals to Swing concerts at Carnegie Hall. He met McGhee for the first time back in North Carolina in 1939.

Walter Brown "Brownie" McGhee was born on 30 November 1915 in Knoxville, Tennessee, and was also disabled – polio having left him with a deformed right leg. His brother, nicknamed "Stick", also became a blues performer – as a child he was often seen using a branch to push the invalid Brownie along in a cart. As a teenager Brownie McGhee worked the circuses and medicine shows, including the Rabbit Foot Minstrels.

Following Blind Boy Fuller's death in 1941, McGhee was billed by record producer J.B.Long as "Blind Boy Fuller II", a name he would later tour with, often backed by Terry (his most successful record in this guise was a tribute to the original, "Death of Blind Boy Fuller"). Nineteen forty-two saw McGhee in New York, where Terry joined him, and the two recorded with Leadbelly for Alan Lomax's Library of Congress project.

Below: The Rev. Gary Davis was born on 30 April 1986 in Laurens, South Carolina. He was a major force in the East Coast/Piedmont blues school and his earthy vocals and elaborate finger-picking techniques were influential on many bluesmen and folk-bluesmen from Blind Boy Fuller to Bob Dylan.

Left: Sonny Terry (right) and Brownie McGhee enjoyed huge success as a musical duo from 1942. Terry was a versatile and entertaining harmonica man, while McGhee was adept at the nimble guitar-picking associated with the southeastern states. They remained together until Terry's death in 1986; although they occasionally pursued individual projects – there was reputedly no love lost between them off-stage – it is as blues ambassadors, stalwarts of the festival and folk-club circuits of the 1960s and '70s, that they will be best remembered.

thereby sealing their partnership.

Remaining in New York, the duo went on to work with many of the leading figures in the white, left-wing folk music movement that was gathering force in the coffee houses and clubs: artists such as Pete Seeger, Woody Guthrie and Cisco Houston. Like other performers, 1942 saw their recording career briefly interrupted by two events: firstly, the passing of a law which greatly reduced the amount of shellac – the raw material used to make gramophone records – permitted for non-military purposes, and secondly, the calling of a strike by the American Federation of Musicians, who feared that the rapidly expanding network of jukeboxes was threatening the livelihoods of musicians. Both bans, however, had been lifted by the following year.

The Reverend Gary Davis – by now singing only religious songs – arrived in New York soon after Terry and McGhee. By the end of the decade he had resumed recording, often backed by McGhee, but it was not until the 1960s,

thanks to the persuasive tactics of a white New Yorker, the guitarist and blues enthusiast Stefan Grossman, that Davis finally agreed to record secular blues and ragtime tunes. In the meantime, Sticks McGhee also came to town in 1947, finding his moment of fame with the song 'Drinkin' Wine Spo-Dee-O-Dee', which became a huge hit in 1952 when re-recorded, with Brownie backing his brother, by the emerging Atlantic label, the first rhythm and blues success for a company that was soon home to a roll-call of the biggest r&b names of the era.

While Terry and McGhee were serving their apprenticeships in the 1930s, Big Bill Broonzy was becoming a star in Chicago, paving the way for Muddy Waters and a generation of southerners traveling north. Before we follow the Delta men up to post-war St Louis and Chicago we should pause to pay tribute to the other forms of the blues taking root elsewhere: the jump-and-jive bandleaders, the blues shouters and the West Coast school among them.

PROFILE

big bill broonzy

Right: Big Bill Broonzy, photographed in the early 1950s. His early career in Chicago proceeded in fits and starts before he became established as the city's major pre-war attraction. In 1939 he replaced Robert Johnson, who had been murdered, at a Carnegie Hall "Spiritual to Swing" concert, and in the 1950s became the best-known bluesman in Europe.

The jaunty, syncopated guitar style of Big Bill Broonzy, his warm, friendly voice and his musical telepathy with the pianist Black Bob, made him the biggest blues star in Chicago in the years leading up to the Second World War, and yet his career had so many false starts that he could easily have been relegated to a footnote in blues history.

Broonzy was a pioneer twice in his long career: he was the first of the great southern bluesmen to become a star in Chicago as well as the first blues performer to spread the message of the music to Europe in the 1950s.

He was born on 26 June 1893 in Scott, Mississippi, though his family soon moved across into Arkansas. In spite of learning to play a home-made violin as a boy, he showed few musical ambitions in early manhood, becoming in turn a farmer, coal miner and First World War soldier, before moving to Chicago in 1920. A meeting there with Papa Charlie Jackson prompted him to learn the guitar, but his first attempts to become a recording star were unpromising: he was turned down by Paramount several times before the label released one of his records and this subsequently flopped.

This gloomy pattern continued until he was recorded for Bluebird in 1934 by which time, helped by his partnership with Black Bob, he had discovered his own easy-going style in the tradition of Leroy Carr and found success at last. From this moment until the end of the Second World War Broonzy became, perhaps,

the most-recorded of all bluesmen.

After the war Broonzy was one of the first blues artists to find success in white folk-music circles, a path already taken by the less charismatic Josh White. By the early 1950s his reputation had spread to the clubs of Europe: he recorded in both Paris and London as early as 1951. But whereas typical Chicago sessions of the late 1940s laid down songs like 'I Love My Whiskey', 'Stop Lying Woman' and 'San Antonio Blues', European session details reveal a slightly different repertoire: 'When Did You Leave Heaven', the old warhorse 'John Henry', and 'Plough Hand Blues' (despite over thirty years having lapsed since Broonzy was last acquainted with a plough).

Although one of the Paris sessions does include altogether grittier stuff like 'Friendless Funeral Blues' and 'Crowded Graveyard', the blues enthusiast Sam Charters has identified "two Big Bills" during the last stage of his career: the Chicago blues singer performing for modern black audiences, and a coffee-bar hero peddling a folk heritage of railroad and sharecropping songs. Broonzy wasn't complaining, however, and both personae appeared to sit well on his broad shoulders.

One unusual result of Broonzy's then-rare crossover appeal was a ghosted autobiography, *Big Bill Blues* (1955); but, tragically, he could not enjoy it long. Having contracted throat cancer he died in 1958. His legacy, in part, was the interest in the blues that developed in Europe in the wake of his visits.

jumpin' and shoutin'

"Have you heard the news?
There's good rockin' tonight"

From 'Good Rockin' Tonight' by Roy Brown

That traveling finishing school for blues musicians, the Rabbit Foot Minstrels, had one graduate who put jump and jive into the music, laying down one of the foundation stones for rock 'n' roll. Louis Jordan took the blues as his raw material, but not to muse on hard times, nor as a vehicle for social comment: his purpose was to ensure that the joint was jumping and that the crowd were laughing, not crying into their beer.

In 1938 Jordan took the plunge and formed the first Tympany Five – a name he stuck with however many musicians he hired – to fulfill a New York residency. The format was that of a Harlem swing combo, slick, finger-popping, and heavily influenced by the most celebrated purveyor of Harlem jazz, Cab Calloway. Jordan brought more boisterousness to the style, establishing himself in 1942 with 'Five Guys Named Moe'. This release came three years into a relationship with the Decca label that was to take him to the early 1950s and the threshold of rock 'n' roll. In 1954 rock 'n' roll's first star, Bill Haley, also began recording for Decca, his 'back-beat' style borrowing heavily from Jordan.

But while it lasted Jordan was the uncrowned "King of the Jukeboxes", with such exuberant hits as 'Ain't Nobody Here But Us Chickens', 'Saturday Night Fish Fry', 'Caldonia', 'Is You Is Or Is You Ain't My Baby?', 'Choo Choo Ch'Boogie,' and 'Open the Door, Richard'.

Left: Louis Jordan was born on 8 July 1908 in Brinkley, Arkansas. He served a long apprenticeship as a clarinet player, saxophonist, singer, and dancer, before taking America by storm with his Tympany Five.

In 1951, just as the big-band era was about to give way to the leaner disciplines of rhythm and blues and rock 'n' roll, Jordan decided to form a big band, an ill-timed decision that was compounded by leaving Decca through the revolving door that was welcoming Haley. Jordan continued to record for various labels, and in the early 1970s put together a new Tympany Five, but his death in 1975 came fifteen years too early to enjoy the remarkable success in London's Shaftesbury Avenue of the "compilation show" *Five Guys Named Moe*, a revue based on his repertoire.

Jordan's music was a response to changing circumstances. As the migration north continued, a significant black urban population grew in the 1930s, still facing rising unemployment, deprivation, and racism, but beginning to find a voice and to express its frustrations through demonstrations that often tipped over into riots. The city blues developed against this shifting social tide. The Depression had stemmed the flow of "classic" blues, and the black orchestras in evening dress were too formal to appeal to the hipper, poorer, more politicized city audience now growing – and becoming restless – in the ghettoes of Chicago, St Louis, Los Angeles, Detroit and Philadelphia. In the late 1930s Jordan established a new style: brash, humorous, confident, and swinging like the clappers.

In Kansas City another style of band blues took root that combined jazz discipline with embryonic r&b riffing; and out in the spotlight a leather-lunged blues "shouter" was snapping his fingers and belting out the song. Pianist Jay McShann's band was one of the best: it included the young saxophonist Charlie Parker as well as the vocalist Walter Brown.

However, war service split up this version of the band, and when McShann was picking up the pieces in 1945 he hired as Brown's replacement another "shouter" with a growing reputation, Jimmy Witherspoon. A spell in the Merchant Marine had meant that among the Spoon's earliest performing credits were gigs with a forces band in Calcutta. Once back home he joined McShann for a four-year stint. The young Witherspoon was much influenced by the

Left: Jimmy Witherspoon was born on 8 August 1923 in Gurdon, Arkansas. He started off as a blues 'shouter' in the mid-1940s in the same mould as his primary influence, Big Joe Turner. This photograph was taken in London in 1976.

Far left: The archetypal blues 'shouter', Jimmy Rushing, pictured here in the early 1950s, was born on 26 August 1902 in Oklahoma City. As a young man he traveled extensively through Texas, the Mid-West, and across to Chicago before making his recording debut in 1929. His most celebrated partnership was with Count Basie with whom he performed regularly from the mid-1930s and with whom he produced some of the most potent 'big band' blues of the era.

Above: Pianist Amos Milburn
was born on April 1 1927 in
Houston, Texas, where he
formed his first band after the
war. His big break came in
1948 when 'Chicken Shack
Boogie' on Aladdin, a rocking
celebration of a long night out,
made him a national star.

"Mr Five by Five" because his height was almost matched by his width, he created the Kansas City style – unsubtle but relentlessly rhythmic – with the blues lyric declaimed against the riffing of the brass section. From the 1930s he often performed with Count Basie until setting up his own group to work in the Savoy Ballroom, New York City, in 1950. Rushing and Basie toured together in the 1960s, however, and he remained utterly faithful to the blues style he had largely created until leukemia struck in 1971, a year before his death.

By the mid-1940s a contrasting style of sophisticated blues was being developed in Los Angeles by Charles Brown, who brought a blue note to the smooth, small-combo jazz that had been Nat "King" Cole's successful trademark since the beginning of the decade. Born in 1920 in Texas City, he won a Los Angeles talent contest in 1944 and joined Johnny Moore's Three Blazers as singer and pianist. Essentially, he was a crooner – intimate and melancholy – and his wistful 'Drifting Blues', cut by Aladdin, is now a standard of the genre.

A third vital strand of pre-rock 'n' roll blues is represented by Amos Milburn, whose professional path often crossed that of Charles Brown. Not strictly a "shouter" – since he worked in a small-combo "jump" setting rather than in front of a big band – but far more rumbustious than the melancholy Brown, Milburn paved the way for generations of rocking rhythm and blues bands belting out twelve-bar endorsements of booze, broads and boogie. He had a big success with 'Let's Make Christmas Merry, Baby' in 1949, while the hits that took him triumphantly into the 1950s – "Bad, Bad Whiskey"; 'Thinking and Drinking'; 'Let Me Go Home, Whiskey'; and 'One Scotch, One Bourbon, One Beer' – shared a festive spirit of a slightly different nature.

1963 found Milburn briefly and surprisingly on the Motown label, but a series of strokes curtailed his career and he died in Houston in 1980. The musical progression, from the blues, through rhythm and blues, and on to rock 'n' roll, started with Milburn. Even Fats Domino, one of the biggest-selling artists of the rock 'n' roll era, although quintessentially a New Orleans

original Kansas City shouter Big Joe Turner (see Profile, page 54) whose style was based on the rhythmic and ensemble disciplines of jazz, and some of Witherspoon's finest collaborations have been with such jazz giants as Ben Webster and Count Basie. In the early 1990s, having defied cancer, he was still carrying the torch for the music with his 1992 album *The Blues, the Whole Blues and Nothin' but the Blues*.

If the image of the blues "shouter" has an archetype, however, it is Jimmy Rushing. Called

player, was undoubtedly influenced by him.

A similar progression, following the history of another upbeat party-invitation song, 'Good Rockin' Tonight', takes us from Roy Brown to Wynonie Harris to Elvis Presley. Although Brown was a "shouter", he sang with a passion and emotional intensity rare in the genre, and thus sketched out the blueprint for James Brown, Jackie Wilson, and the later soul singers of the 1960s, as well as for blues performers in the B.B.King and Bobby "Blue" Bland style. He was born on 10 September 1925 in New Orleans but his blues was unmistakably West Coast, having been nurtured in the gospel-group tradition of Los Angeles. In 1945, success in talent shows secured him a contract with the Gold Star label, and 'Good Rockin' Tonight', cut by DeLuxe in 1947, set the pattern for a series of hits which peaked in 1950 with the wild, naked emotion of 'Hard Luck Blues'.

Sadly, Brown could neither fit into the rock 'n' roll era nor ride it out. Although his attempts included cover versions of Buddy Knox's Texan rockaballad 'Party Doll' and Fats Domino's 'Let the Four Winds Blow' in 1957, both of which were modest r&b chart successes, neither restored his fortunes. However, in 1970 Brown's career was somewhat revived when he joined Johnny Otis' rhythm and blues revue which scored a success at the Monterey Jazz Festival, thereby bringing him greater public recognition in the years before his death in 1981.

By the time Brown made his first records, Wynonie Harris, who was born on 24 August 1915 in Omaha, Nebraska, had already been a star for several years. Indubitably a "shouter", Harris moved from the Mid-West to Los Angeles in the early 1940s and joined Lucky Millinder's band, first recording with them in 1944. With a style based on sheer, hoarse lung-power, but with an intuitive feel for blues phrasing, his first hit was 'Who Threw the Whisky in the Well'. Harris worked with numerous bands during the rest of the decade, notably those of Johnny Otis, Illinois Jacquet, and Lionel Hampton, and in 1948 he covered Roy Brown's 'Good Rockin' Tonight' on the King label, swiftly returning the song to the top of the r&b charts.

In the early 1950s Harris scored again with 'Sittin' On It All the Time' and 'I Like My Baby's Pudding', both laden with double entendre, but like Roy Brown, he did not weather the rock 'n' roll storm particularly well, and in his later years ran a bar, making only occasional comeback appearances before his death in 1969. The passion of Brown and the raucous power of Harris were two vital precursors of rock 'n' roll, however, and when Elvis Presley cut his loose-limbed, lascivious version of 'Good Rockin' Tonight' as his second Sun single in 1954, the genetic line was acknowledged.

Johnny Otis is one of the most interesting and unusual figures in West Coast blues. A Californian-born Greek, he is not remembered particularly as a musician – although as a drummer he was good enough to record with the great jazz saxophonist Lester Young in 1945 and for a few years he toured with Louis Jordan – but everything else in the blues he has done: bandleader, club-owner, impresario, manager, songwriter, disc-jockey and talent scout. In the 1950s he toured with his R&B Caravan, and his extraordinary gift for spotting talent is manifested by a selective list of the singers featured in his revue: Esther Phillips, the Robins (who later were transformed into the greatest of the rhythm and blues vocal groups the Coasters), Big Mama Thornton (originator of 'Hound Dog' in a version produced by Otis), Johnny Ace (whose biggest hit 'Pledging My Love' was similarly produced by Otis), Jackie Wilson, Hank Ballard, and Little Willie John.

In the 1970s Otis worked with another of the pioneers of blues-based r&b singing, Roy Milton. Milton, born in Wynnewood, Oklahoma on 31 July 1907, formed his group, the Solid Senders, based in Los Angeles, in 1938. In 1946 they had a huge hit with 'RM Blues', a boogie-based riff that established Milton, alongside Jordan and Milburn, as an important figure in the journey towards rock 'n' roll. These musicians were playing small-combo r&b with brass and keyboards to the fore, but a technological innovation was soon to switch emphasis to the guitar.

The electric blues began tentatively when an acoustic guitar was first married to a micro-

phone in the 1930s by jazzmen such as Eddie Lang and Django Reinhardt. Meanwhile, others to be intrigued by the possibilities were, significantly, Les Paul and the Texan T-Bone Walker, respectively the inventor of the solid electric guitar and its earliest great blues exponent.

Paul was an electronics freak and white country guitarist who formed his Les Paul Trio in 1936. In 1940 he attached guitar strings to a railway sleeper and created "the log" in which sound was amplified by tiny microphones, or pick-ups, rather than by resonating as it does in the hollow body of a conventional guitar. However, a slab of timber was clearly a work in progress, and Paul was actually beaten to the next major step – a marketable, solid-body, electronic guitar – by rival boffin Leo Fender, who produced his Broadcaster model in 1948. Paul replied in 1952 with his own version, the Les Paul, sold through the Gibson company, by which time Fender's guitar had been renamed the Telecaster. These two models set the standard, as they and the later Fender Stratocaster still do today. The first hit to reveal the potential

of this new style of guitar was Arthur Smith's 1947 'Guitar Boogie', a Fender tour de force, soon to be followed by Paul's own extraordinary performances like 'Lover', released in 1948, and in 1951 – in a celebrated partnership with his wife, Mary Ford – 'How High the Moon'.

With its opportunities for sustained and bent notes – quite apart from its ability to lead a band over the noise of a crowded bar – the electric guitar could have been made for the blues. T-Bone Walker set the style. Born Aaron Thibeaux Walker in Linden, Texas, on 28 May 1910 and growing up in Dallas – he was yet another of Blind Lemon Jefferson's guides as a boy – he toured with medicine shows and revues from his early teens, selling himself on his versatility; although he majored on guitar he was proficient on any number of instruments, and could also sing, dance and tell jokes.

As a flamboyant showman he thus founded a long line of blues entertainers – Chuck Berry, B.B.King, Buddy Guy, and Johnny "Guitar" Watson are obvious examples – who have taken an intimate, reflective form of music and turned it into "show time" without losing the fire or the passion that are at the heart of the blues. In T-Bone's pioneering electric solos of the 1940s, fluid, inquisitive, and inventive, one can hear the genesis of so many later styles: Berry's "chicken-pecking" technique across adjacent strings, for example, or B.B.King's virtuoso flights.

T-Bone first recorded in 1929 at a time when he was also working with Cab Calloway's band. By 1934 he was in Los Angeles where he began experimenting with guitar amplification, and at the end of the decade he was playing mainly with an orchestra led by Les Hite with residencies in New York and Chicago. Nineteen forty-two saw him back in Los Angeles recording for Capitol, whose 1940s portfolio included the classic slow blues that is always associated with him, 'Stormy Monday', and his signature piece, 'T-Bone Shuffle'. On the latter, the stabbing piano of Willard McDaniel biting into the shuffle rhythm sounds like one of the earliest sources of Jamaican blue beat, while Walker lays down the pattern for innumerable twelve-bar workouts that would be imitated by later musicians. For

Above: T-Bone Walker was one of the very first electric bluesmen. He also had a reputation for showmanship, often performing exhibitionist tricks like doing the splits, playing the guitar behind his neck, and prowling the stage with a long guitar lead.

the last twenty years of his career, often struggling with his fitness, Walker worked the clubs and festivals, and recorded regularly. His epitaph is an intriguing double album, *Very Rare*, produced in 1973 by Jerry Leiber and Mike Stoller, which teams him with jazz men, like Dizzy Gillespie, Zoot Sims, and Gerry Mulligan, and such contrasting pianists as New Orleans' James Booker and the Texan Charles Brown. Walker died at home in Los Angeles in 1975.

Hard on his pioneering heels came Lowell Fulson, a man who, like Walker, had native American blood and whose apprenticeship included traveling through Oklahoma and Texas with Texas Alexander. From his country blues origins Fulson has made a longer musical journey than anyone featured in these pages: to the West Coast in the 1940s where his fellow musicians included Ray Charles; to the Chicago label Chess in the 1950s for his biggest hit, the instantly memorable, dark-brown 'Reconsider Baby'; to 1960s soul (he wrote and recorded the original version of 'Tramp', hilariously revived by Otis Redding and Carla Thomas); to the obligatory collaborations with white rock session superstars (his album *In a Heavy Bag* survived the marriage far better than similar experiments by either Muddy Waters or Howlin' Wolf); and finally to "grand old man" status. Thus one of the earliest of the electric blues players – with a spiky, more attacking approach than Walker – was still to be seen playing clubs in the 1990s having outridden or absorbed every subsequent development in the music.

With the electric blues underway we must now return to our central journey, from the Delta via Memphis and St Louis to Chicago. Pianist Leroy Carr and his guitarist partner Scrapper Blackwell, though more intimately associated with Indianapolis, were active in St Louis in the early 1930s. Following their 1928 hit 'How Long Blues', a subtle and affecting marriage of Carr's plangent piano style and cool, restrained voice with Blackwell's neat guitar lines, they were both hugely successful and influential. Theirs was a sophisticated, urban approach to the blues, with both instruments having equal weight, and the partnership flourished until Carr's death from the effects of alcoholism in 1935.

Peetie Wheatstraw arrived in east St Louis in 1929, a guitarist, pianist and singer who had been born in Ripley, Tennessee, on 21 December 1902, and who was certainly aware of the Carr and Blackwell style. His was a darker, more brooding approach – as is suggested by his best-known nickname, "The Devil's Son-in-Law", or an alternative billing as "The High Sheriff from Hell" – but he was a compelling performer, and recorded successfully in New York and Chicago as well as St Louis, enjoying a decade of hits with songs such as 'Crazy with the Blues', 'Good Whiskey Blues', 'Peetie Wheatstraw Stomp' and 'Throw Me in the Alley'. He died in 1941 when his car collided with a train at a crossing in St Louis, a few yards from his home

Fellow passenger Big Joe Williams survived the crash. Born on 16 October 1903 in Crawford, Mississippi, he was therefore in the earliest generation of bluesmen, but he survived to perform until the late 1970s and died in 1982. He is best remembered, perhaps, for two things: his unique, strident, nine-string guitar and his 1935 recording 'Baby Please Don't Go', one of the best-known of all blues songs. Williams, who, like so many of his contemporaries, was schooled as an itinerant entertainer and tent-show musician, wandered throughout the South before making the journey north to St Louis and on to Chicago. In the 1960s, as a member of the traveling Folk Blues Festival, his fame spread to Europe and he was one of the first and last of the great traditional blues singers.

Below: Johnny Otis, born in Berkeley on 8 December 1921, was a bandleader, impresario, manager, songwriter, disc-jockey, and talent scout. He grew up in a black neighborhood and opened a club, the Barrel House, in Los Angeles in the late 1940s.

blues

PROFILE

big joe turner

When Bill Haley ushered in the rock 'n' roll era in 1954 with his cover of 'Shake, Rattle and Roll', the song was but a shadow of the rumbustious original by Kansas city blues "shouter", Joe Turner. It was no doubt a source of amusement to the song's composer, however, that the most obscene metaphor, about "a one-eyed cat peeping in a sea-food store", was so well coded as to escape the blue pencil.

One result of Haley's hit was that for a while Turner himself was packaged as a rock 'n' roller, prompting him to record follow-ups such as 'Flip, Flop and Fly' and 'Lipstick, Powder and Paint'. To him, after all, rock 'n' roll was simply "a different name for the same music I been singing all my life".

Turner's form of big-band Kansas music was distinct from a typical southern blues: the latter was confessional, intimate, whereas Turner stood in front of a band and belted, his voice one of the instruments. Born on 18 May 1911 in Kansas City, he built a reputation in the early 1930s as a singing bartender (Kansas City had an administration with an unusually liberal attitude to Prohibition). Later, Turner sang with local bands, including that of Count Basie, before teaming up with the great boogie-woogie pianist Pete Johnson. Local celebrity and the influence of talent scout John Hammond Senior led to a booking on the 1938 "Spirituals to Swing" concert at New York's Carnegie Hall, an event which established both men.

Having recorded for numerous labels in the 1940s Turner's "rock 'n' roll" phase began when

he signed to Atlantic in 1951: 'Sweet Sixteen' was released in 1952, followed by the rock 'n' roll anthem 'Shake, Rattle and Roll' in 1954. Undimmed by his commercial success, Turner's blues credentials were stressed in the classic 1956 album, *Boss of the Blues*, which was released at a time when he was also featuring in the pop charts. In fact, Turner's muscular style was an obvious bridge between jazz, blues and rock 'n' roll, and he bestrode it confidently. Toward the end of his career, now based in New Orleans, he alternated between making records and performing on the burgeoning festival circuit. He died on 23 November 1985.

chicago plugs in

"The blues had a baby and they named it rock 'n' roll"

From 'The Blues Had a Baby' *by Muddy Waters*

Chicago was never going to be the "sweet home" of Robert Johnson's optimistic fantasy. In the ghettos of the North, racism was more subtle than it had been back home. As late as the 1960s, Mayor Richard Daley, perhaps the last of the old-style "city bosses" without whose patronage nothing thrived, was denying that ethnic enclaves existed in Chicago. In fact, planning regulations and building patterns had effectively, if covertly, ensured segregation since the move north began in earnest in the 1920s.

In 1966 Dr Martin Luther King arrived on one of his many rallies, raising awareness of inequalities in housing, health, education and the other basics of a civilized society. In the South, Dr King's South, racism was ingrained, but even though the victorious North had ended slavery, there remained bigots who had to seek other paraphernalia with which to clothe their sentiments – newsreels of Dr King's Chicago rally show clear footage of Dr King and his supporters moving serenely through a forest of swastikas.

In the South poor blacks and poor whites lived side by side – physically if not in brotherhood – and it is striking that all the great names of white country music who were born into such a background, like Jimmie Rodgers, Hank Williams and Carl Perkins, invariably credited a black neighbor as their musical mentor. As Willie Dixon has recalled, "They didn't have all-black areas in the South." But in the early 1960s, when my generation of white British fans was greeting our hero Muddy Waters, his name meant nothing to most white

Left: Willie Dixon, New Orleans, 1987. Born in 1915, Dixon,
a talented bass-player and composer, learnt verse
structures from his mother, who was a poet. Having failed to
sustain a career as a boxer, he turned to music in 1939.

Chicagoans living a mile away from him on the other side of the tracks. It took the Rolling Stones to effect the introduction.

Meanwhile in the Chicago ghettos of the 1940s a musical revolution was brewing, a northern, urban, electric translation of the Delta blues, on street corners, in bars and clubs, and on a growing number of record labels. In the steady process whereby Chicago was becoming the leading northern outpost of the blues, the arrival in town of Muddy Waters in 1943 was the most significant since that of Big Bill Broonzy and Washboard Sam in the 1930s. Waters is profiled later in this book in recognition of the fact that he was the single most influential figure on those white blues musicians of the 1960s who, in turn, were able to refocus the spotlight on the great originals.

If Muddy Waters was the star attraction in the Chicago blues circus, then Willie Dixon was the ringmaster. When he published his ghosted autobiography in 1989 he took as its title a song he had written twenty years earlier, and it is hard to dispute its arrogant claim: "I Am the Blues". He was born at the southern tip of the Delta, in Vicksburg, on 1 July 1915 and has cited Victoria Spivey's 'Black Snake Blues' as his first musical memory.

His mother first moved to Chicago in 1926, but by the end of the decade Dixon was back in

Mississippi. When he returned north in the early 1930s he worked as a professional boxer for a while before learning to play stand-up bass. It was as a member of the Big Three Trio, working locally in the late 1940s, that he began to back blues artists on record. This included work for the Aristocrat label, renamed Chess by owners Leonard and Phil Chess in 1950 and scoring its first hit with Muddy Waters' 'Rollin' Stone'. Dixon's versatility served the label well. The brothers Chess knew far more about business than they did about the blues, and so Dixon was vital to them as producer and a&r man, talent scout, and songwriter, session player and arranger.

Even if Dixon had only been a songwriter his role in Chicago blues would be secure: he is credited with over 500 titles, including the Muddy Waters hits 'Hoochie Coochie Man', 'Just Make Love to Me' and 'I'm Ready'; Howlin' Wolf's 'Little Red Rooster' and 'Spoonful'; Otis Rush's 'I Can't Quit You Baby', and the irresistible 'Wang Dang Doodle', a hit for both Etta James and Howlin' Wolf. There are twenty-seven versions of his Little Walter hit 'My Babe' listed in his autobiography, by artists as diverse as Lightnin' Hopkins and Ricky Nelson. In the 1960s Dixon appeared on the American Folk Blues Festival tours of Europe, set up a booking agency and continued recording and club work

In the early 1980s it was finally deemed that Led Zeppelin's 'Whole Lotta Love' was stolen from Dixon's 'You Need Love', a 1962 Muddy Waters track. Zeppelin had already recorded Dixon's 'You Shook Me' and 'I Can't Quit You Baby', duly credited, but had settled earlier court cases for "borrowing" his 'Bring It on Home' and rewriting 'Killing Floor' as 'The Lemon Song'. "The white man has control of everything that the black man had made in America, so that makes him the owner," said Dixon. "Naturally, they didn't write the history of the guy who made it – they wrote the history of the guy who got it." Dixon used the settlement money to set up his Blues Heaven Foundation, established to help underprivileged musicians. He died in 1992.

It was one of Dixon's performers, Howlin'

Above: Chuck Berry, whose ingenious compositions redefined the boundaries of rock 'n' roll.

Right: Bo Diddley's r&b based rock 'n' roll was influential to many bands, including the Rolling Stones.

Malcolm Chisholm, "...one of the greatest musical talents I've ever come across... bone-stupid... he had the paranoia of a very stupid man."

Dixon has told the story of dragging the Wolf off stage and holding him up against a wall by the collar trying to instill some sense into him: the picture of two mountainous men discussing etiquette in the wings is a daunting one. Late in his life, when he visited England, the Wolf's personality, as well as his voice, still dominated the clubs he played in, even though by this time he had given up rolling around the stage screaming, with the veins pumping in his neck, choosing instead to remain seated: a dignified old man, barely under control.

Ike Turner recorded the Wolf for the Memphis label Sun – then a little-known blues imprint yet to discover Elvis Presley, Jerry Lee Lewis, Johnny Cash and Carl Perkins – and the label's owner Sam Phillips leased the tapes, 'Saddle My Pony' and 'Worried All the Time', on to Chess in Chicago. The move to Chicago, and the final break with tractor-driving, didn't come until 1953, a cautious two years after his first hit 'How Many More Years'.

Until then the Wolf had sometimes played guitar as well as his more familiar instrument, a rudimentary but effective harmonica, but when he signed with Chess he was teamed with Hubert Sumlin, the peerless guitarist who contributed the instantly recognizable riffs to many of Howlin' Wolf's strongest tracks, like the pounding 'Smokestack Lightnin''. This 1956 hit soon became a rhythm and blues standard, while the Wolf/Dixon classic 'Little Red Rooster' gave the Rolling Stones a 1964 number one. In 1970 the Wolf and Sumlin recorded in London with their white heirs – Eric Clapton, Stevie Winwood, Bill Wyman, and Charlie Watts among them. 'Dogshit' was the Wolf's opinion of this musical marriage. He died in 1976.

In the mid-1950s the ghetto clubs of Chicago were home to Chess stars: Muddy Waters, Jimmy Rogers, Little Walter, Otis Spann, the second Sonny Boy, the Wolf, and Hubert Sumlin; while Jimmy Reed and Eddie Taylor were on Chess's main rival Vee-Jay. Albert King was also in town for a couple of years; John Lee Hooker

Wolf, who, more than anyone else, transported the power and passion of Charley Patton, Son House and Robert Johnson to Chicago. Given that Dixon himself was physically huge and possessed unusual leadership qualities, some of his comments on the Wolf make it clear that this bull-necked slab of a man was a frightening presence. "Howlin' Wolf was pretty rough to deal with", he remembers. "It required a lot of diplomacy working with him." Similar sentiments were expressed by Chess recording engineer

Left: Little Pat Rushing jamming on Maxwell Street, Chicago. Many of Chicago's greats, including Bo Diddley, were graduates of the thriving street-corner musical scene that was already centered on Maxwell Street. Today the street continues to provide a forum for would-be professionals – a place for busking; assembling a repertoire; waiting for the big break.

63

Right: Jimmy Reed was born in Dunleith, Mississippi, on 6 September 1925. For most of his career he played with childhood friend and fellow guitarist Eddie Taylor, a technically more proficient and habitually more sober musician than Reed, who helped to coax Reed's undisciplined sound into a more commercial form.

and Lowell Fulson were regular visitors; and the young Otis Rush, who had lived in Chicago since 1948, was forming his first band.

And then, in 1955, two Chess signings changed the rules. The sophisticated Chuck Berry and the anarchic Bo Diddley took Chicago into the rock 'n' roll age, linking hands metaphorically with Little Richard in Los Angeles and Fats Domino in New Orleans as the

first and the greatest generation of black rockers. In 1955, the year before 'Heartbreak Hotel', the revolution arrived. These were bluesmen playing the blues as it had never been heard before. The 1957 Bo Diddley recording 'Before You Accuse Me' symbolizes one aspect of this new power. He cut it only once and his guitar is hopelessly out of tune, but no-one seemed to notice: the performance was utterly magnetic and became a rock 'n' roll standard.

Many of the strands of Chuck Berry's style existed separately: the jazz lines of guitarist Charlie Christian, the blue notes and stage antics of T-Bone Walker, the warm, confidential swing of Charles Brown and Nat 'King' Cole, the drive of Muddy Water's band. Berry combined these into a youthful music and added his own lyrical discipline. Suddenly a bluesman was focusing on the concerns of the newly-invented "teenager" (a species that had presumably always existed, but which had only recently been emancipated by the increasing spending power of a nation now fully recovered from the Second World War). He was writing, moreover, with the ingenuity of Gershwin or Cole Porter. Bob Dylan would certainly have been a different songwriter if Berry had not shown him how to weld together rhythm, imagery, and rock 'n' roll exuberance.

Berry's first hit, 'Maybelline', exalts that new god, the fast car, not just as a sexual metaphor but as a liberator. When his souped-up Ford takes on a Cadillac the sentiments are far from environmentally sensitive, but he proves himself the daddy of the Beach Boys, the hot-rod boys, and the 1960s truckers. The high priest of the mechanical church, James Dean, who died in 1955, would have loved it.

Charles Edward Anderson Berry was born in St Louis, before Peetie Wheatstraw arrived there, on 18 October 1926 in the first age of radio. In his 1987 autobiography – which though revealing shows that his precision with a rock 'n' roll lyric does not translate into prose – he lists the artists whose records particularly influenced him as a teenager, thereby providing an intriguing snapshot of early 1940s black radio. He recalls: "Tampa Red, Big Maceo, Lonnie Johnson, Arthur Crudup, Muddy Waters [although Berry would probably not have encountered Waters until later in the decade], Lil Green [a Mississippi singer who began recording with Broonzy in Chicago in 1940], Bea Boo [presumably Beatrice Booze, best known for her version of the classic 'See See Rider'], Rosetta Thorp [gospel singer Rosetta Tharpe], and later, Louis Jordan, T-Bone Walker, Buddy Johnson, Nat

Cole and Charles Brown." He was also influenced by white swing bands and says that the recording of 'Tommy Dorsey's Boogie Woogie' determined him on a musical career.

In the early 1950s Berry formed a local trio with Ebby Hardy and also Johnnie Johnson, whose distinctive piano style decorates Berry's finest records. Arriving in Chicago in 1955 he was pointed toward Chess Records by Muddy Waters, and 'Maybelline' was released in the same year. It carried with it a writing co-credit to disc-jockey Alan Freed, whose Cleveland radio show "Moondog's Rock 'n' Roll Party" is usually acknowledged as popularizing the term "rock 'n' roll", an example of how a record could be "assisted" by a disc-jockey in return for a financial stake. It certainly worked: the record reached the top of the r&b charts. Berry's 1956 releases included 'Roll Over Beethoven', and by the end of the 1950s he had created many of the masterpieces of the rock 'n' roll era, including 'Rock 'n' Roll Music', 'Sweet Little Sixteen', 'Johnny B Goode', 'Carol', and 'Sweet Little Rock 'n' Roller'.

Having served a jail sentence in his youth for armed robbery, Berry was back in prison in the early 1960s for "transporting a minor across a state line for immoral purposes", an elaborate charge he has always denied. He emerged to find himself the idol of the new generation of English bands like the Beatles and the Rolling Stones, and continued releasing wonderful songs: 'Memphis Tennessee', 'No Particular Place to Go' and 'Nadine' are among his best, and no one who witnessed his 1964 UK tour with Carl Perkins could ever forget its excitement. There has always been a darker side to his character, however – exemplified by further tangles with the law and a meanness of spirit that often tarnishes his stage performances – but the bridge he built between the ghetto music of Chicago and mainstream rock 'n' roll makes him one of the most important figures in the story of popular music. All the same, he was not the only architect of that bridge: Bo Diddley emerged at the same time.

Bo Diddley was born in McComb, Mississippi, on 30 December 1928. His father's name was

Right: Albert King. In the 1970s, in both Memphis and New Orleans, King established a new sound for the blues: a fluent guitar spiralling out of a soul or funk setting. He died in 1992.

Far right: Sam Maghett was born in Mississippi in 1937, but grew up in Chicago. With Little Brother Montgomery on piano, he cut 'All Your Love' in 1957, the first of just a handful of great recordings on which his reputation rests. Just before his death in 1969 his fame was beginning to spread to Europe, and his West Side sound lives on in the work of Otis Rush and Buddy Guy.

Bates, but he was adopted by a family named McDaniel who moved to Chicago in 1934 and grew up as Ellas Bates McDaniel. Having learned the violin, he taught himself to play the guitar using an open tuning that later helped to give his music its distinctive rhythmic pulse. He acquired his nickname at school, though he can't remember how, and was working on the streets from the age of thirteen, at one stage calling his band the Langley Avenue Jive Cats, members of which included his school-friend Earl Hooker, who would later become a distinguished blues guitarist in his own right.

From 1951 onwards Bo came in from the cold and found work in clubs, and in 1955 he made a demonstration record with his long-time partners, Jerome Green on maracas and harmonica player Billy Boy Arnold. The two songs on this record, 'Bo Diddley' and 'I'm a Man', became his first release on the Chess subsidiary, Checker, reaching number two in the r&b charts. His eponymous anthem is based on the rhythm that immediately became his trademark, an insistent, percussive beat, sometimes represented as

"shave and a haircut, six bits", which Johnny Otis was also using on the West Coast (notably on his 1958 hit 'Willie and the Hand Jive').

Although Bo returned to the rhythm many times, and often chose to star in his own songs, there is far more to his music than variations on the 'Bo Diddley' theme. He was a pioneer of electronic trickery, using reverb, fuzz and distortion ten years before Jimi Hendrix, and he played bizarre – oblong and fur-covered, for example – custom-made guitars. His songs vary from semi-improvized, humorous raps like 'Say Man', in which he and Green trade insults, to the chilling 'Who Do You Love', in which a man who can walk along forty-seven miles of barbed wire and who is in the habit of riding a lion into town is still tormented by jealousy. His repertoire includes nursery rhymes and doo-wop, straight blues and frantic rock 'n' roll, but he could never be mistaken for anyone else.

In spite of this he was a major influence on other artists. Out in west Texas, Buddy Holly made a garage version of 'Bo Diddley', while 'Who Do You Love' spawned hugely contrasting

Right: Freddie King, pictured here in the early 1970s, performing one of the strident guitar solos which had such a profound influence on Eric Clapton. He died in 1976 from heart failure and bleeding ulcers. He was only forty-two.

covers: a manic nightmare by Canadian rocker Ronnie Hawkins and a lengthy hippie doodle by Quicksilver Messenger Service. The early Rolling Stones repertoire contained as much Bo Diddley as anything else; the Pretty Things took their name from one of his songs; the Animals told 'The Story of Bo Diddley'; and in 1979 punk band the Clash invited him to tour with them. Today, as he approaches old age, his bespectacled, portly demeanor contrasting with the raw jungle noise of his music, Bo Diddley is still a compelling performer.

The chief Chicago rival to the Chess label was Vee-Jay, founded in 1953 by Vivian Carter and James Bracken. They built a stable which included doo-wop groups like the Spaniels and the Impressions, and for a time – like Chess and several other labels – John Lee Hooker; but above all, from the year the label began until 1965, they had Jimmy Reed.

Reed arrived in Chicago with Eddie Taylor in 1949 and launched Vee-Jay with the first Reed single 'High and Lonesome'. Their r&b hits began in 1954 with 'You Don't Have to Go', but it is Reed's cross-over into the Hot Hundred that makes him so unusual: a dozen times, from 1957 to 1963, he entered the pop charts, and his last hit 'Shame, Shame, Shame' also scored in the UK, making him another icon of the British blues bands, who faithfully learned his 'Bright Lights, Big City' and 'Big Boss Man'.

And yet Reed never contrived to present an "Uncle Tom" image or to clean up his blues in an effort to make it palatable to white audiences: he did exactly the opposite. Throughout his life, his Mississippi drawl remained uncompromised to the point of being incoherent, and he made no attempt to combat his alcoholism until late in life, finally drying out in the 1970s only to succumb to a heart attack in 1976. In addition to Taylor, whose distinctive guitar figures added the decoration to Reed's languid rhythm, he had another important collaborator in his wife "Mama", who wrote many of his songs and often sang with him; although, for the most part, she is clearly acting as a prompt rather than a harmonizer, quite often simply standing beside Reed whispering the next lyric line in his ear.

There was variation in his records – rhumbas, attractive melodies like 'Honest I Do', slow blues and rockers – but many followed a similar pattern: the shuffling rhythm (often another clear forerunner of the Jamaican blue beat) is established, topped by Reed's shrieking harmonica and Taylor's guitar, then Reed slurs through two twelve-bar verses, followed by a twelve-bar instrumental break, then a third verse, and, finally, a fade out. That's it – and it is irresistible – one of the great sounds of the blues.

Before recording with Vee-Jay, Reed occasionally worked with Albert King. Although King made his recording debut in 1953, he spent the rest of the decade working in the South outside music, playing only part-time, before re-appearing in a St Louis studio in 1959. His time was to come a decade later when, with the deep soul of the southern studios now the most vibrant branch of black music, King injected blues power into the Memphis soul label Stax, recording with Booker T and the MGs to make the album charts with 1967's stunning 'Born Under a Bad Sign'.

Another King, Freddie, was born in Gilmer, Texas, on 3 September 1934. He absorbed the Texan legacy, from Blind Lemon Jefferson to T-Bone Walker, and arrived in Chicago in 1950. His first recording as a solo artist was 'Country Boy' on El-Bee in 1956, but his particular fame rests on a series of fast-fingered, attacking instrumentals – 'Hideaway' (1960), 'The Stumble' (1961), and 'Driving Sideways' (1962), in particular – that became essential source material for British followers like John Mayall, Eric Clapton, and Peter Green. King was a big man, a flashy performer with huge bejeweled rings glinting on every finger, a showman who continued to be a favorite in the UK until his death from a heart attack, sadly young, in 1976.

Magic Sam died even younger, having pioneered the so-called "West Side" sound of Chicago blues which, though its most celebrated practitioners were all southern immigrants, was distinct from the Mississippi "South Side" sound of Muddy Waters and the Delta men usually found on Chess. Magic Sam recorded in a back room for the storefront label, Cobra, a neurotic

blues
PROFILE

b.b.king

Below: B.B.King, pictured here in the mid-1950s, moved the blues into the sophisticated mainstream without destroying its soul. Indeed, his deep feel for the music, expressed with stunning technical expertise, has provided a master-class for most of his blues and rock successors.

On 21 November 1964 the crowd roared their appreciation as one of the most commanding voices in the blues strode into 'Every Day (I Have the Blues)', the opening number on Live at the Regal, recorded at Chicago's Regal Theater. It was an unforgettable moment. and the sensuous, unmistakable sound of B.B.King's guitar, Lucille, and the crowd's expectant response, still have the power to thrill. This is "the King" holding court, and such is his seasoned showmanship – he gave 342 performances in 1956, for

example – that a B.B.King concert can rarely be a disappointment.

King, like James Brown, follows a tradition of black show-business revue that goes back at least as far as Ma Rainey – with confident, well-honed introductions taking the place of between-song mumblings. Tuxedos and flashing rings replace dungarees, but King's depth of feeling as a bluesman prevents all this from becoming some sanitized cabaret, just as the military precision of a Brown concert cannot hide his soul power.

For a career in the blues the young Riley B. King had impeccable credentials. He was born on a plantation on 16 September 1925 near Indianola, Mississippi, where he sang in a church choir from the age of four and later in a school gospel group. His mother died when he was nine and he left school to work on a plantation, before teaching himself to play the guitar and forming another gospel group at the age of fifteen. He began to play the blues to entertain fellow soldiers during the war, and in 1946 moved to Memphis where his reputation was established, initially as a member of the Beale Streeters with Bobby Bland, Johnny Ace and Earl Forrest.

This apprenticeship led to his being billed as the Beale Street Blues Boy, shortened to Blues Boy, and hence to B.B. He combined local gigs with disc-jockey work on Memphis radio station WDIA, and first recorded in 1949 for the Bullet label. Although his guitar style – with clean clusters of notes commenting on each lyric line, sustained "bent" notes, and subtle use of light and shade – soon became very much his own, the early influence of electric-guitar pioneer T-Bone Walker is clear.

The hits began with 'Three O'Clock Blues' in 1952, and for the next decade King recorded and toured constantly, bolstering his reputation by sheer hard roadwork. By the time he arrived for his Regal Theater engagement in 1964 he was the biggest name in the blues, better known in America even than Muddy Waters.

King's appeal spread to white audiences in the late 1960s, helped by a Rolling Stones tour in 1969, and in that year one of his most celebrated blues, 'The Thrill Is Gone', was a pop Top Twenty hit. In the mid-1970s he was reunited with Bobby Bland, by now another star with cross-cultural appeal. A list of his collaborators in the latter half of his career, from jazz-funk band the Crusaders to Irish superstars U2, is confirmation that his musicianship transcends the confines of the blues, and in the 1990s he continues his punishing concert schedule, proving himself as at home in New York's Apollo Theater as in London's Royal Festival Hall. The thrill is far from gone.

Below: B.B.King, pictured in New Orleans in 1992, is dedicated to live performance. Since the 1950s he has worked 300 nights a year to earn himself the title "King of the Blues", and thanks both to his musical eloquence and to his masterful performances he has been one of the blues' most effective ambassadors.

britain gets the blues

"Can blue men sing the whites
Or are they hypocrites to sing the blues?"

From 'Can Blue Men Sing the Whites?' *by the Bonzo Dog Doo Dah Band*

When Muddy Waters first came to Britain in 1958 his audience was unprepared for his stinging slide guitar and his emotional body language – the raw red meat of his unadorned electric blues. Hitherto, their only experience of the "real thing" had been the deliberately toned-down folksy acts of artists like Big Bill Broonzy, footage of whose 1956 European tour in Brussels – with its moody lighting, drifting cigarette smoke, candles in wine bottles, and polite applause – includes his rendition of a sentimental ditty called 'When Did You Leave Heaven'. It is beautifully sung, but not the typical musical fare of a noisy Chicago club. As Bob Dylan found eight years later, amplification alone could offend British folk fans.

Acceptance of Waters, the godfather of Chicago blues, by white audiences on both sides of the Atlantic came in stages: Carnegie Hall in 1959, Newport Jazz Festival in 1960, a record deliberately calling Muddy Waters a folk singer in 1963, all preceded his triumphant return to Britain in 1964 as the star of a blues caravan.

Even then, when the tour reached Bristol's Colston Hall and this writer's eager ears, a clock-watching caretaker echoed the opinion of critics in 1958 when, on the stroke of 10 o'clock, just as Muddy was warming up, he switched off the electricity. However, in most places the battle had been won in those six years and Britain was now an outpost of the electric blues empire.

Right: Cream (from left to right: Ginger Baker, Jack Bruce, and Eric Clapton) were a blues-based "supergroup" who were not built to last. During two stormy years, however, they forged a pattern for the stadium rockers of the 1970s.

Right: John Mayall proved to be the catalyst of some of the finest ever British rhythm and blues line-ups. In the 1960s his band, the Bluesbreakers, provided a training ground for many young British musicians who went on to greater things. Eric Clapton, Mick Taylor, and Mick Fleetwood were just a few of the rock stars of the future to graduate from Mayall's line-ups.

Moreover, thanks to the enterprise of the Pye record company, who regularly leased and re-leased Chess material, it was the Chicago artists who became Britain's particular heroes. The major label EMI also put out blues material on their catch-all American imprint, Stateside, and introduced British listeners to Hooker and Reed, as well as to the southern delights of Slim Harpo, Lazy Lester, and Lightnin' Slim.

One man, above all, strove to educate 1950s Britain in the ways of the blues and that was bandleader Chris Barber. However, he was not alone: fellow jazz men Ken Colyer and Humphrey Lyttelton, in particular, were also enthusiasts, and Lyttelton's rollicking 1956 hit 'Bad Penny Blues' still sounds like the most exciting home-grown record of the entire decade. But Barber it was who brought Broonzy and Waters, Sonny Terry and Brownie McGhee to Britain and who employed blues enthusiasts Lonnie Donegan and Alexis Korner in his band.

In 1962 Korner and harmonica player Cyril Davies, tired of skiffle, formed Blues Incorporated, among whose personnel were at times bass player Jack Bruce and drummer Charlie Watts. In the meantime, Dick Taylor, who was to become a founder member of the Rolling Stones, was rehearsing in southeast London with Mick Jagger and Keith Richards. Brian Jones, who introduced himself to Korner, also played occasionally with Eric Clapton and Tom McGuinness in a Surrey band, the Roosters, as well as with the unrelated Paul Jones. The nucleus of the London rhythm and blues movement was coming together.

In 1962 there was a split between Korner and Davies – Korner, perhaps, being more attracted to the jazzier bluesmen like Lonnie Johnson, while Davies was a Chicago man at heart – which left Blues Incorporated now consisting of Korner, Bruce, drummer Ginger Baker, organist Graham Bond, and pianist Johnny Parker. Meanwhile, Davies formed his All Stars – with vocalist Long John Baldry and most of Screaming Lord Sutch's backing band, the Savages – but, alas, died of leukemia before his role in the blues revival could be indelibly established. He left behind a virtuoso harmonica single, 'Country Line Special', and his band became the Hoochie Coochie Men, with Rod Stewart joining Baldry on vocals.

From the floating population of Blues Incorporated arose the Rolling Stones, named after Muddy Waters' 1950 hit and assembled by Brian Jones, with Jagger, Richards, Taylor, and pianist Ian Stewart. Early drummers included Mick Avory, later of the Kinks. Soon, Taylor opted to return to art college; but with Bill Wyman and Charlie Watts on board the band gained a residency at the Crawdaddy club in a southwest London pub and a manager in Andrew Loog Oldham. He hustled them a Decca contract, and the Stones recorded Chuck Berry's 'Come On' as their first single. Stewart, whose bank clerk image didn't quite fit this scruffy answer to the Beatles, was eased off-stage but remained the "sixth Stone" until his death in 1986. In the meantime, this rebellious crew – who, nevertheless, meekly agreed to replace Berry's reference to "some stupid jerk" with the less defiant "some stupid guy" – moved uptown from the Crawdaddy where their residency was

inherited by the former Metropolitan Blues Quartet, now the Yardbirds, managed by Crawdaddy promoter Giorgio Gomelsky and soon to include Eric Clapton.

By 1964 the London blues scene was established. John Mayall, on Korner's advice, had moved down from Manchester and had swiftly recruited Clapton when the guitarist became disenchanted with the increasingly commercial Yardbirds. Meanwhile, in the Yardbirds, Clapton was succeeded in turn by Jeff Beck and Jimmy Page; former Stone, Dick Taylor, had re-emerged from art college as a Pretty Thing; future Stone,

Below: Mick Jagger, who was a fringe member of Alexis Korner's Blues Incorporated before setting up the phenomenally successful Rolling Stones with Keith Richards in 1962. By 1965 the Stones had made four albums and nine hit singles, and by the end of the decade had changed from rock 'n' roll rebels to leading members of the new rock aristocracy.

Ron Wood, was cranking out twelve-bars in the Birds; Georgie Fame was resident at Soho's Flamingo Club; south London's Groundhogs, led by Tony McPhee, were John Lee Hooker's choice of band when touring Britain; and Graham Bond had formed his Organization, which included saxophonist Dick Heckstall-Smith, as well as Ginger Baker and Jack Bruce, who would later join Clapton in the first supergroup Cream.

In Birmingham the Spencer Davis Group, built around the prodigious talents of "Little" Stevie Winwood, were rooted in the blues, as were Belfast's Them (Van Morrison's father was an enthusiastic blues collector) and Newcastle's Animals. The pop charts were full of blues-based bands, among them the Kinks, who released a squawking cover of Little Richard's 'Long Tall Sally' before Ray Davies found his own songwriting voice, and Manfred Mann, whose members Paul Jones and Tom McGuinness later returned to their 'roots' as the Blues Band.

The UK charts also welcomed the great originals: Hooker with 'Boom Boom'; Reed with his 'Shame, Shame, Shame'; Howlin' Wolf's 'Smokestack Lightnin''; and, in 1964, one of the finest Chess records to be produced after the label's golden decade, organist Tommy Tucker's 'Hi Heel Sneakers'. This sly, fluid twelve-bar was instantly adopted by the British bands, even though the jokey footwear of the title, along with references to the lady's "wig hat", sounded a little strange when enunciated by white vocalists. Tucker toured Europe in 1965 with the Animals, one of Britain's biggest bands at the time, as his backing group. The follow-up record, 'Long Tall Shorty', was also a modest hit and was swiftly covered by the Graham Bond Organization as their debut single.

Europe, and Britain in particular, also became a home from home for John Lee Hooker, Jimmy Reed, Muddy Waters and the blues caravan tours, Howlin' Wolf, Chuck Berry, Bo Diddley, Sonny Boy, and many other bluesmen, while the twelve-bar ruled in innumerable pub back rooms. Tom McGuinness, hired as a backing musician because as well as being a member of one of the UK's most successful bands he was also a fan, remembers an occasion before a per-

formance when Arthur "Big Boy" Crudup, unrewarded author of two early Elvis Presley hits, arrived to play and took out of his suitcase his old "stage suit", the back of which had been gnawed away by rats.

The enthusiasm for the blues is well-illustrated by the 1964 bill at the Richmond Jazz and Blues Festival, as recalled in Bob Brunning's book *Blues in Britain*. In these pre-Woodstock days a weekend event like this was pleasantly low-key and civilized, a forty-eight-hour, open-air concert rather than an endurance test fit for an SAS initiation. Friday night arrivals could hear the Grebbells (a Gomelsky band which included founder Yardbird, "Top" Topham); the T-Bones, fronted by a fine singer in Gary Farr; the Authentics; and the Rolling Stones. Saturday featured Ronnie Scott, Chris Barber, Dick Morrissey, Long John Baldry's Hoochie Coochie Men, Memphis Slim, and Jimmy Witherspoon; while the Sunday bill was Kenny Ball, Humphrey Lyttelton, Graham Bond, Georgie Fame, Mose Allison and the Yardbirds. Brunning reminds us that a ticket for the three days cost one pound. The weather wasn't too good, but the music made up for it, and it ended with a jam session featuring the Yardbirds, Fame, and Bond.

What was it about the blues that particularly appealed? After all, apart from occasional bull's-eyes by Cliff Richard, Johnny Kidd, and Billy Fury, young British musicians had failed to make much sense of rock 'n' roll – even in its white version, which after all had its roots in British and Irish folk music. Instead they happily welcomed Eddie Cochran and Gene Vincent as semi-residents in the late 1950s, and soon started playing Elmore James licks instead.

As Tom McGuinness recalls:

Pop music had got so bland. Elvis was in the army; Jerry Lee Lewis was singing country; Chuck Berry was in jail; Little Richard had gone back to the church. What we had instead was Johnny Tillotson and Bobby Vee. Rock 'n' roll had gone soft, lost its energy, power, vitality. I was playing in a band with school friends in Wimbledon and I remember saying in 1962 that I wanted to play r&b. They thought I was mad: they insisted that

Left: Fleetwood Mac. This classic line-up existed from 1968 to 1970 and included: (clockwise from front) Peter Green, John McVie, Danny Kirwan, Mick Fleetwood, and Jeremy Spencer. The band was set up in 1967 by Peter Green when he, McVie, and Fleetwood quit John Mayall's Bluesbreakers. Their first album *Fleetwood Mac* featured straight ahead blues and was a steady seller for over a year. Green then added Danny Kirwan as third guitarist for their third album, *Then Play On,* released in 1969. Many consider this line-up to be the band's best. Over the next twenty years this highly successful band would be reorganized no less than eight times.

what people wanted was Shadows tunes.

But at the same time there was all this wild music you could hear on the American Forces Network, and sometimes on Radio Luxembourg. It seemed alive and exotic. I think that black music always seemed exciting to white fans at the time, just because it was different. It was a gradual thing, though, to discover the blues. No road to Damascus. We'd already heard Chuck and Bo. I'd seen James Cotton playing with Chris Barber. And so one gradually learned where the music came from – like hearing Chuck Berry do 'Worried Life Blues' and tracing it back to the piano player Big Maceo. I've always thought that Chris Barber's contribution to this process has been underrated. He was bringing these people over and it some-times seemed that I was the only one who wanted to hear them! But he persisted, and gradually the blues caught on because it was the most exciting thing that was happening at the time.

Below: The Yardbirds, left to right: Paul Samwell-Smith, Chris Dreja, Jim McCarty, Jeff Beck, and Keith Relf. The original line-up included Anthony "Top" Topham on guitar, soon replaced by Eric Clapton. Despite, at various times, including three of the best British guitarists of the era, Eric Clapton, Jimmy Page, and Jeff Beck, the band only thrived for five years. However, their influence was longer lasting and paved the way for the psychedelic heavy rock of the late 1960s and '70s.

Black music took root not just in Britain's increasingly cosmopolitan capital city but also in the ports, where sailors would often sell the lat-est records in return for drinks money. Them emerged in Belfast; the Animals in Newcastle; in Liverpool the Searchers and the Beatles (who founded their early repertoires on Detroit and New Orleans records); and in Bristol traditional jazz flourished. Record shops, such as Dougie Knight's in Belfast, Dave Carey's Swing Shop in Streatham, south London, and Dobell's in London's Charing Cross Road were among the meccas to which the faithful gravitated.

In 1966, when they made the outstanding *Bluesbreakers* album, John Mayall's sidemen were Clapton, bass-player John McVie, and drummer Hughie Flint (who was later to join McGuinness in McGuinness-Flint). Jack Bruce occasionally replaced McVie, and when Clapton went walkabout – most notably a two-month working holiday in a vague attempt to introduce the blues to Greece – deputizers were future Stone, Mick Taylor, and Peter Green. When Ginger Baker also became a temporary Bluesbreaker the seeds of Cream were sown.

This group was unveiled in July 1966, by which time Mayall had decided that he wanted Green as Clapton's successor. A year later, with Mick Fleetwood now the Bluesbreakers' drum-mer, Mayall's band was once again a seedbed for future rock bands, this time for Peter Green's Fleetwood Mac, made up initially of Green, Fleetwood and Bob Brunning (who was soon replaced by John McVie).

The blues heritage of Cream is undeniable. Clapton has been quoted as saying he intended it to be like Buddy Guy with a rhythm section, with himself, one assumes, cast in the Guy role, while Jack Bruce and Ginger Baker undoubtedly favored a more democratic approach. The results took the band away from the blues but created a fascinating fusion centered more around the songs of Jack Bruce and his writing partner Pete Brown than in Clapton's greater celebrity. Jazz, r&b, psychedelia, and straight-forward pop went into the mixing bowl, while old blues songs were either given a heavy-rock treat-ment, like Robert Johnson's 'Crossroads', or as

Left: Phil May of the Pretty Things, a band with a dirty, driving rhythm and blues image in the same vein as the Rolling Stones. After a handful of mid-1960s hits they faded for a while before re-emerging with a "rock opera", that predated the Who's *Tommy*. called *S.F.Sorrow*.

in the case of Skip James's 'I'm So Glad', were totally refashioned. The results on stage could often be exhilarating, but it was an alliance not built to last. 'I Feel Free' was the biggest of the band's seven hits, but interestingly even that didn't quite invade the Top Ten. In 1968 Cream played farewell concerts in America and London, and by the end of the year had split up.

Meanwhile, the tireless John Mayall and his Bluesbreakers – described by Clapton as a "great school for musicians" – are still going strong nearly thirty years later. And though his other most notable graduates, Fleetwood Mac, were to become unrecognizable in the 1970s – when they all but abandoned the blues to evolve into one of the most successful bands in the world – in their early years they played the best white blues of all.

The strength of Peter Green's playing lay in his timing, his intuitive sense of what to leave out, the nerve to leave spaces in his solos, as well as the technical ability to persuade his fingers to play what his mind dictated. At the end of the decade another hugely successful British blues group, Ten Years After, demonstrated the opposite approach with guitarist Alvin Lee, a technician of staggering dexterity, cramming his solos with as many notes as his flashing fingers could manage. It was exhilarating stuff, but often one pined for Green's considered but emotional style: his version of Little Willie John's 1955 blues ballad 'Need Your Love So Bad' is one of the finest of white blues achievements.

Had this book been written a year earlier, Peter Green as a musician might have remained in the past tense, but after years of drug-induced psychiatric problems he made some tentative but heart-warming reappearances in 1996 for festival performances. Now back on the road, he may never be restored to full mental health, but even a rusty and slightly confused Green is still a fascinating guitar player.

When they released their first album in 1968, produced by blues label-owner Mike Vernon and with guitarist Jeremy Spencer adding his earthy Elmore James slide guitar to the sound, Fleetwood Mac were riding such a wave of blues

Below: Graham Bond. Following the defection of Jack Bruce and Ginger Baker to Cream in 1966, the Graham Bond Organization never regained its stride, and although Bond continued to record and perform, the last few years of his life were plagued by money problems, excessive drug use, and a fascination with the occult. He died in 1974.

popularity that it went immediately to the top of the album charts. In the same year their chart-topping single, 'Albatross', an atmospheric instrumental that beautifully evoked the gliding flight of the huge bird over empty oceans, was an early hint that this band, too, were not simply blues revivalists; and when Green abruptly disappeared into apparent oblivion in 1970 the end of the "purist" band was near. It arrived when Spencer made an equally sudden exit a year later, in his case to join the controversial American religious sect, the Children of God.

Most British blues bands of the 1960s – and there were hundreds of them – attacked the music with more enthusiasm than subtlety. Even the celebrated Yardbirds, guitar heroes notwithstanding, found it hard to translate the excitement they could generate on stage into the recording studio. Needless to say, the British musicians – and it is notable how many of them came from the leafy middle-class suburbs around London – could never actually become Mississippi bluesmen, and were thus never able to express the blues experience as if it was their own. They could not cruise brand-new Ford Thunderbirds along endless highways; neither could they take the night flight down south to the Delta. Instead they went to Brighton by British Railways and played the slot machines on the pier. Hardly the stuff of blues.

Yet, what emerged from the fusion was a frantic, hard-driving, exuberant, rhythm and blues sound that made up with sheer noise what it lacked in authenticity. Moreover, it was more an underground than a commercial force – the band that inspired Van Morrison to become a rhythm and blues singer, for example, the eccentric Downliners Sect, never had a hit – although the best of the bunch did manage to score in the charts several times.

If Dick Taylor had stayed as the Rolling Stones's bass player then the Pretty Things might never have happened, but he emerged from Sidcup Art College with new enthusiasm and a co-conspirator in singer Phil May. Their first major success in the summer of 1964 was the snarling 'Rosalyn', followed by two more big hits, 'Don't Bring Me Down' and 'Honey I Need'.

Though the band keeps re-forming, even in the 1990s, the raw energy of their early sound ran out – they were soon dabbling in the dreaded "concept album" form – but it was exhilarating while it lasted.

This electric noise was not the only strand of British blues: in the folk clubs, acoustic blues was being played with equal enthusiasm. Davey Graham was a former Mayall musician with a very individualistic guitar style founded in the blues which came to be known as "folk baroque", other exponents of which were Bert Jansch and John Renbourn. Jansch, whose early influences included Broonzy and Lightnin' Hopkins, became one of the leading "singer-songwriters" of the 1960s, while Renbourn, another veteran of r&b bands, took his early enthusiasm for the blues on a journey toward traditional English music, a fruitful combination.

Down in south London there was a nucleus of blues enthusiasts that included Dave Kelly and his sister Jo-Ann. Dave became a particularly adept exponent of bottleneck guitar, as a solo folk-club act, as leader of his own bands, and, for the past fifteen years or more, as a member of the Blues Band. Jo-Ann was quite simply one of the world's great female blues singers. Had she had ambitions for stardom, something she always seemed to back away from at the last moment, there were American record producers eager to place her in the same company as Janis Joplin and Bonnie Raitt. Memphis Minnie was a particular favorite of hers, but her husky, expressive way with a lyric was all her own. One of her most moving live performances on record is an *a cappella* rendition of one of the songs quoted at the beginning of this book, 'Death Have Mercy'. Tragically it didn't, and this marvelous artist died of a brain tumor in 1990.

There was undoubtedly a "blues boom" in Britain in the 1960s, brought about by a combination of factors, namely the evangelistic enthu-

Above: The Animals, formed in 1962, originally comprised, left to right: John Steel, Alan Price, Chas Chandler, Hilton Valentine, and Eric Burdon. The band was said to have been given their name by local audiences in response to their wild appearance and Burdon's frenzied stage act.

siasm of father figures, such as Barber and Korner; the stagnation of commercial pop in the early part of the decade; the willingness of mainstream record companies to release blues records; and an equal willingness on the part of blues performers to find new fame in old age. However, it would be wrong to say that, like other fashions, the blues revival was followed by bust. The blues is not the twist or punk rock; along with its white equivalent it is the root of rock, and, as such, is here to stay.

Among those who took homegrown blues into the 1970s were Chicken Shack, Savoy Brown, and the Irish guitarist, Rory Gallagher, whose band, Taste, inherited Them's residency at the Maritime Hotel in Belfast. Gallagher's earliest musical influence was Lonnie Donegan, Chris Barber's banjo-player and the 1950s skiffle king, but he soon developed a guitar style rooted in the Chicago West Side sound of Buddy Guy. With Taste his biggest success was the 1970 album, *On the Boards*. From 1971 until his premature death in 1995 Gallagher led his own bands, a blues guitar hero not just in Ireland but throughout Britain and Europe as well.

In London, and subsequently in licensed premises throughout the country, the so-called "pub rock" movement of the 1970s was firmly based in the blues, rhythm and blues, and country. The mainstream of pop music had moved into vast, impersonal stadiums and had become dull and stagnant once more, and the saccharine drone of the Carpenters, Abba's bland Europop, and the posturing of "glam rock" ruled the charts. But in the pubs the blues played on; and some of the best bands, like Canvey Island's Dr Feelgood, became popular enough to move on to a bigger stage.

Today, in Britain, there are still blues festivals in many provincial towns: pianist Diz Watson plays the music of New Orleans with such an authentic touch that the residents of that city are happy to accept him as one of their own; and in the Midlands the Big Town Playboys turn the music of heroes such as Louis Jordan and Amos Milburn into one of the most dynamic acts in the country. The blues remains alive and well in Britain.

Left: Rory Gallagher was born in Ballyshannon in County Donegal in 1949 and raised in Cork where he played in local bands until he was fifteen. Later, with Charlie McCracken on bass and John Wilson on drums, he formed Taste, a high energy blues-rock trio that moved to London in 1968. Gallagher died in 1995.

blues PROFILE

alexis korner

Above: Alexis Korner in the 1950s before he set up Blues Incorporated.

While British jazz men like Chris Barber espoused the blues in the 1950s, and Lonnie Donegan introduced the work of Leadbelly to a British audience, the greatest single figure in the "blues revival" of the early 1960s was the former Barber sideman, Alexis Korner. As a good-natured and helpful talent-spotter, enthusiast and evangelist for the music he was unparalleled. From the Rolling Stones to Free and Led Zeppelin, innumerable bands owed their start, in part at least, to Korner. His deep, husky voice also brought him fame as a radio presenter helping him to spread his enthusiasm for the music, and in 1978 his fiftieth birthday party, which was filmed for television, attracted a plethora of British blues talent, including Eric Clapton, Zoot Money, Chris Farlowe, and Paul Jones.

Born in Paris on 19 April 1928, Korner succumbed to cancer on New Year's Day 1984. He had joined Barber's band on guitar in the late 1940s, and with Barber and Donegan played in the skiffle group that was featured as part of Colyer's act in the 1950s. He first recorded with harmonica player Cyril Davies and guitarist Jeff Bradford in 1957, and in 1961 opened a blues club in Soho featuring Blues Incorporated, his hugely influential band, which became a staging-post in the early careers of so many stars. The band's 1962 album *R&B from the Marquee*, with Korner playing a miked-up acoustic guitar in country-blues style, influenced a generation.

Having given birth to the Stones, Korner added Jack Bruce and Ginger Baker to his roster of sidemen. They moved on to John Mayall

and later to the supergroup, Cream. Korner's approach to the blues was catholic enough to embrace straightahead jazz players, like tenor Art Theman, and a former member of impresario Larry Parne's stable of instant pop stars, Duffy Power, who threw off the teen-idol trappings to reveal his skill at playing harmonica, as well as handling Blues Incorporated's vocals.

In the late 1960s Korner formed other groups including Free at Last before finding brief chart success with the big band, CCS. His radio work expanded into advertising voice-overs during the 1970s, and toward the end of his life he appeared in Charlie Watts's band Rocket 88 with Jack Bruce and Ian Stewart. Anyone who has been involved with British blues remembers the avuncular, generous Korner with affection, respect and gratitude.

Above: Korner performing in London in 1969. By this time he had helped an entire generation of British bluesmen to success, and had established a varied career for himself as performer and broadcaster.

south
and west

"I got my suitcase in my hand
Ain't that a shame?
I'm leaving here today
Yes I'm going home to stay
Yes I'm walking to New Orleans"

From 'Walking to New Orleans' *by Fats Domino*

We have followed the Mississippi north from its so-called Delta, and must now head in the opposite direction to Lake Pontchartrain, on whose southern shore stands the "Crescent City", New Orleans. From there we will wander into Louisiana and further west, paying tribute to more of those artists who did not take part in the better-known migration from Mississippi to Chicago.

Because of its commanding strategic position at the mouth of the vast Mississippi–Missouri river courses, New Orleans has a long history of conquest and confiscation by territorially minded Europeans. Having been established by the French in 1717 on the east bank of the river, and named for the French regent, the Duc d'Orléans, it was declared the capital of Louisiana in 1722 before being ceded to Spain in 1763. Meanwhile, on the west bank of the river, in the area known as Algiers, the French quarter – architecturally a product of French and Spanish-Caribbean influences – was evolving an identity all of its own.

In 1800 Louisiana as a whole was returned to the French before being sold on to the USA in 1803. Thirteen years later, during the American War of Independence, it was the site of a formidable British defeat by the armies of

Right: Fats Domino, pictured here performing in London in 1978, has always remained faithful to the New Orleans rhythm and blues sound he pioneered in the 1950s.

General Andrew Jackson – despite the fact that, unknown to both sides, a truce, in the form of the Treaty of Ghent, had been signed by Britain and the USA a few weeks earlier – and in 1862 there was a second Battle of New Orleans, this time during the American Civil War, which placed the city under the control of Union forces.

Its checkered history made New Orleans a more cosmopolitan city than many in the growing Union: its white citizens were mainly French, Spanish, Irish, German and Italian; its black population was from Africa, from the Caribbean, and from the slave plantations; its characteristic Creole people were of mixed French and Negro descent. Nowhere was this multiculturalism more evident than in the city's music, which found expression through French opera companies and Creole orchestras; dance bands and ragtime ensembles; street entertainers and brothel pianists; brass bands and ceremonial marching bands.

For the best part of this century it has remained a vibrant musical center, home to a range of sounds, from Dixieland jazz to rhythm and blues, from rock 'n' roll to funk. One of the city's street buskers, the blind twelve-string guitarist Snooks Eaglin (born on 21 January 1936), who became world-famous in the late

Right: Lightnin' Slim was one of the first "Baton Rouge" bluesmen to be recorded in the post-Second World War period. He was born Otis Hicks on 13 March 1913 in St Louis but raised in Louisiana, moving to the Louisiana town of Baton Rouge in 1946. Here, his 'Bad Luck Blues' was recorded for the Feature label in 1954, becoming one of the first records to bring the raw, swamp blues that had long been popular locally to a wider audience.

1950s, is a living repository for virtuoso blues, ballad, ragtime and narrative song. But, somewhere in this fusion – and in the strutting exhibitionism of the marching bands – developed a common characteristic in the form of the New Orleans rhythm of the "second line" in which an extra syncopated beat is added to each bar.

One result of this is that however successful a New Orleans sound may have become commercially, in other parts of America and indeed internationally, it remains indelibly of that city. Part of the excitement of the blues, of rhythm and blues, and of rock 'n' roll, certainly in the days before there was an "international" music as characterless as "international cuisine", is that at heart the music retained its parochial identity.

No one demonstrates the envigorating regional nature of New Orleans blues more forcefully than Fats Domino. In the 1950s, Fats

Above: Professor Longhair, at the Newport Jazz Festival in 1973. His individual and unorthodox piano style mixed blues, cajun, calypso, jazz, ragtime, and zydeco to produce a sound that has become synonymous with New Orleans.

Right: Dr John (real name Mac Rebennack) is a multi-talented New Orleans bluesman, who has devoted his skills as a musician, songwriter, arranger, producer, and talent scout to the development of the New Orleans sound from the late 1950s to the present day. This photograph was taken at the New Orleans Jazz Festival in 1985.

became one of the biggest record-sellers of all time, up there with Elvis Presley, Bing Crosby, and the Beatles; and yet he has always sounded exactly, and delightfully, what he is: a Creole piano-thumper from a New Orleans club.

Antoine "Fats" Domino was born in the Crescent City on 10 May 1929 into a musical family, and at the age of sixteen was playing the piano in a local band. In 1949 he began his long and extraordinarily fruitful partnership with producer, songwriter, and bandleader Dave Bartholomew, and a rolling eight-bar boogie on the Imperial label called "The Fat Man" established the pattern, with warm, sly vocals delivered in a distinctive Creole accent, a pounding piano, and with a booting saxophone solo by Herb Hardesty kicking out of the arrangement. From then until 1963 Domino was never out of the charts: the r&b list at first, the Hot Hundred pop chart from its inception in 1955, the UK hit parade from 'I'm In Love Again' in 1956.

Musical segregation was still such that in 1955 a clean-cut, soul-free reading of Domino's 'Ain't That a Shame' by crooner Pat Boone comfortably outsold the original, having access to more radio stations and slicker distribution. But before long, Domino had turned the tables by transforming ballads like 'My Blue Heaven' and 'Blueberry Hill' into rich slabs of New Orleans rhythm and blues which sold by the million.

His slower songs featured the distinctive "triplet" figures on the right hand, dismissively called "that cling-cling-cling jazz" by the wonderful but rock 'n' roll-hating musical satirist, Stan Freberg. The invention of this technique has been credited by some critics to the blues pianist Little Willie Littlefield, born on 16 September 1931 in Houston, Texas, who had an r&b chart hit in 1949 with 'It's Midnight' and was the first artist to record the Leiber–Stoller classic, 'Kansas City', under the title 'K C Loving'. He was the main influence on Britain's Big Town Playboys, mentioned in the previous chapter, and his "cling-cling-cling" became a characteristic sound of bluesy 1950s r&b and doo-wop. Vocal group the Platters, for example, built a hugely successful career on it.

A move to the ABC–Paramount label in 1963 was the beginning of the end for Domino's unbroken chart run, but there was a nice twist in 1968 when he had a hit with the Beatles' song 'Lady Madonna', a complex McCartney boogie which was undoubtedly written with Domino in mind. There was a further modest chart entry a decade later with the humorous 'Sleeping on the Job', although by this time Domino's reputation and commercial power had long been independent of chart status. He has always employed great musicians, and when on good form he can still put on a show capable of lighting up the most staid of venues, invariably ending with his trademark gimmick of shunting the piano across the stage with his substantial midriff.

Domino was undoubtedly the most successful purveyor of bluesy New Orleans rock 'n' roll, but of course his music did not spring from a

Below: Clifton Chenier, performing at the New Orleans Jazz Festival in 1982. Born on 25 June 1925 in Opelousas, Louisiana, he was the acknowledged "king of zydeco" during the 1960s and '70s. He spearheaded a huge growth of interest in the dance music of those Louisiana musicians who were descended from French settlers, paving the way for the international celebrity of such artists as Rockin' Dopsie.

---

vacuum. He joined a long tradition of piano entertainers from the city, many schooled in the red-light district. One such was Champion Jack Dupree, born on 4 July 1910, who moved to New York in the war years and was particularly important in introducing this musical style to Europe (having, from 1960 onward, settled in turn in Switzerland, Denmark, England, Sweden and Germany). He worked with Korner, Mayall, and Clapton, and his last album, released in 1990, two years before his death, was with the Big Town Playboys. However, he was equally entertaining alone with a piano, a string of stories, and some downhome barrelhouse blues.

The extrovert Cousin Joe Pleasants and Archibald (Leon Gross) were in the same tradition, but undoubtedly the most innovative of the New Orleans keyboard men was Henry Roeland Byrd, who began trading as Professor Longhair with his Shuffling Hungarians, a name whose vaudeville surrealism is worthy of the rubber-limbed English comic, Max Wall. He was born in nearby Bogalusa on 19 December 1918, and the unique piano style he developed in the late 1940s symbolized the city's musical melting pot: an amalgam of blues and boogie, rhumba and calypso that has been at the heart of New Orleans piano playing ever since. Longhair wrote and recorded a series of anthems for the city like 'Tipitina', 'Bald Head', 'Big Chief', and 'Go to the Mardi Gras', and when, in the 1970s, New Orleans established an annual "heritage" music festival, Longhair became its natural star. He died in 1980.

His spirit has lived on, above all, in the music of the white musician "Mac" Rebbenack who was born on 21 November 1941. He is better known as Dr John, the name he adopted in the late 1960s when he reinvented himself as "the Night Tripper", a character purveying a heady mixture of New Orleans r&b, voodoo, and Bayou psychedelia. He was active in the late 1950s as a

Right: Clarence "Gatemouth" Brown, at the New Orleans Jazz Festival in 1987. A versatile musician – he plays the drums, mandolin, harmonica, and bass as well as the guitar and fiddle – Brown developed an eclectic sound that combined jazz, country, and cajun music with the blues.

Left: Bonnie Raitt started playing the blues in the late 1960s in Boston bars and clubs. She was signed by Warner Bros in 1971 and with them produced several albums. By the mid-1980s her career seemed to be on the wane but in 1989 was revived by *Nick of Time,* released on Capitol, which has sold two million and won a handful of Grammys. She remains one of the few female rock musicians to command the respect of the bluesmen.

teenage songwriter, producer and musician, creating such classic rockers as Jerry Byrne's nervy, staccato 'Lights Out' (1957), and in the 1960s was a central figure in a network of expatriate New Orleans musicians working on the West Coast. Dr John suffered for a long time from the effects of heroin addiction, during which period his concert appearances were something of a lottery, but he remained a worthy exponent of the New Orleans musical tradition, exemplified on his 1972 album, *Gumbo,* which carries on the Longhair tradition.

In Louisiana, beyond New Orleans, some of America's most exciting music is to be found, including a rich, swampy version of soul sung by artists like Cookie and the Cupcakes and Tommy McLain; the blues of Lightnin' Slim, Guitar Slim, Slim Harpo, and Lazy Lester; and also the distinctive French-Canadian-Louisiana dance music known as cajun, or zydeco.

Lightnin' Slim (Otis Hicks) was actually born in St Louis on 13 March 1913, but moved south at the age of thirteen. In the post-war years he was active in the Baton Rouge area, and in the

Below: Slim Harpo was an artist who epitomized the Louisiana swamp bluesman. He started performing in the 1940s. In 1955 he got the chance to record with Lightnin' Slim for Excello, thereafter becoming one of that label's most prolific and remunerative artists.

1950s worked with Slim Harpo, recording for the Nashville-based label Excello. By the mid-1960s he had relocated to Detroit where he died in 1974. His blues is often in the lazy, laid-back style of Jimmy Reed but he was also a master technician and an important influence on the work of Buddy Guy.

Even more of a model for Guy was Guitar Slim, who was born Eddie Jones in Greenwood, Mississippi, on 10 December 1926. He was one

of the most impassioned of the great southern bluesmen. Early in his career he worked in New Orleans in a trio with Huey "Piano" Smith, who was later to create a rock 'n' roll classic with 'Rockin' Pneumonia and the Boogie Woogie Flu'. (Smith was also the pianist on New Orleans hits by artists such as Little Richard, Smiley Lewis and Lloyd Price.) Guitar Slim's own recording career began on Imperial in 1951, but his particular classic – recorded for Specialty in the mid-1950s with Ray Charles among the session-men – was the slow, intense 'The Things That I Used To Do'. Buddy Guy's dramatic arrival on the Chicago recording scene in 1960 with 'First Time I Met the Blues' was redolent of Guitar Slim's melodramatic style.

Slim Harpo (James Moore) hailed from Baton Rouge where he was born on 11 January 1924 and died in 1970. He was a singer and harmonica-player, hence the stage name, and, like his brother-in-law Lightnin' Slim, he recorded his handful of irresistible classics for the Excello label, epitomizing the langorous, downhome feel of the Louisiana blues on such sly successes as 'I'm a King Bee' (later covered by the Rolling Stones), 'Raining in My Heart', and 'Baby Scratch My Back'. In similar Jimmy Reed-style, and working with the same group of local artists, was another Baton Rouge Excello artist, Lazy Lester (Leslie Johnson), born on 20 June 1933. Although his stage name reflected the Louisiana lope of his music, he capitalized on it with titles like 'They Call Me Lazy' and 'I'm So Tired'.

Following the Treaty of Utrecht in 1713 the French settlers in Acadia, to be renamed Nova Scotia, were expelled by the British. They sailed down the North American shore to the Gulf of Mexico, settling finally in the fertile land of Louisiana. Their language was a distinct variation of European French, a creole dialect which characterized their music. In the past two decades the indigenous Louisiana music known as 'cajun' has become widely popular, predating the greater recognition given to the musical genres which are generally lumped together as "world music".

In the nineteenth century the accordion became popular in the "cajun" region, taking its place with the violin and guitar. The music was on the one hand domestic and on the other formal. However, during the present century, and in particular with the growth of the record industry, it has developed its familiar exuberant, "good time", dance style which takes its tempo from waltz, two-step or square dance, echoing its distant European parentage in the same breath as borrowing explicitly from local country music or rhythm and blues.

It would be wandering too far from the theme of this book to examine cajun music in detail, so we will represent it instead with one of its finest and most versatile practitioners. Clifton Chenier was born in Opelousas, Louisiana, on 25 June 1925, and before his death in 1987 he had seen cajun move from the parish to the world stage. He is identified with the black version of the music, zydeco, a curious collision between the French two-step dance and the blues. The appeal of his music began to spread in 1950, when 'Squeeze Box Boogie' (a succinct summary of his style) was a hit in Jamaica; but it was twenty years later that his music began to be recognized far more widely as such an envigorating regional style, comparable, say, to Tex-Mex or bluegrass. "Let the good times roll" might have been Chenier's slogan, and indeed it is the title track of his 1960s album, *Bon Ton Roulet*.

It is just a step from Chenier to the blues of Louisiana entertainer Clarence "Gatemouth" Brown, a virtuoso on both guitar and violin, and perfectly capable of playing any other instrument in his band. He was born in Vinton on 18 April 1924, and in the early 1940s became the drummer in a touring revue, William Benbow's Brown Skin Models. In the mid-1940s he was based in Texas, and by the end of the decade had formed his own big band. The fact that Brown is a black man in a cowboy hat reflects the extraordinary range of his music over the past five decades.

Continuing a westward journey to Los Angeles brings us to guitarist and singer Bonnie Raitt, born there on 8 November 1949, who became a key figure in spreading the message of the blues in the late 1960s and '70s. Raitt was a white performer with a foot in both camps – the

white-dominated rock recording industry and the music of her elderly black heroes – and, like the Rolling Stones a decade earlier, she used her access to the white market to evangelize the blues. Raitt was particularly inspired by Robert Johnson; her other influences are listed in *Who's Who* as being Son House, Fred McDowell, and Sippie Wallace, all three of whom she played with in the early 1970s. House and Johnson, as we have seen, were among the first of the Delta

Above: Screamin' Jay Hawkins has had a more successful career on stage than on record, but such classics as the macabre 'Feast of the Mau Mau' and the unrelenting 'Constipation Blues' are essential listening.

Below: Sonny Boy Williamson (Rice Miller) was a harmonica player who found celebrity in the 1940s when he had a regular slot on the Arkansas radio show King Biscuit Time. On moving to Chicago after the death of his namesake he became one the city's biggest names in the 1950s. He later became a colorful participant in the blues revival of the 1960s.

bluesmen to establish this richest of blues styles, while Sippie Wallace looked back to the era of the "classic" blues. Although McDowell (1904–72) was born and died in Tennessee his nickname "Mississippi" identifies him, too, with the Delta. From the 1930s until his rediscovery in the 1960s he was a farmer during the week and a bluesman at weekends; but, like Son House, the celebrity he achieved late in his life has enriched our experience of the music. Raitt is included here – although her white contemporaries feature in the next chapter – because of her direct contact with these early pioneers.

Although each strain of the blues is usually characteristic of the area in which it evolved, occasionally a performer transcends mere geography. Jalacy "Screaming Jay" Hawkins may as well have come from Mars as Cleveland, Ohio, where he was born on 18 July 1929. At the age of twenty, Hawkins became the middleweight boxing champion of Alaska, although history does not record the standard of competition in the frozen north. In 1952 he joined the touring band of Tiny Grimes, and a year later he made his first solo record, 'Baptize Me In Wine'.

It was following a move to the Okeh label in 1956 that Hawkins' individuality began to flower. His most famous song, 'I Put a Spell on You', was later to become a hit for Nina Simone and Alan Price, but the original treatment of this distinctive waltz was too weird for the charts. Hawkins growls and shrieks, threatens and cajoles in a manner which is uniquely pitched between dark, violent passion and camp humor.

There have been humorous blues singers before and since, and the music has a long tradition of showmanship stretching back to Ma Rainey. Hawkins took it to hilarious, eccentric, eye-popping extremes, emerging from a coffin at the start of his act, brandishing a skull-topped cane, dressed in flowing cape, declaiming strange voodoo chants, setting off explosions. The Coasters claim to have once nailed down the lid of his coffin as he waited in the wings, and his act that night consisted of a propped-up casket with a microphone in front of it. A string of artists – most obviously Screaming Lord Sutch, Arthur Brown, Alice Cooper, and numerous heavy metal acts in the Kiss vein – have stolen elements of his act, but the great original has a trump card: beneath the surreal humor and stage antics is a rich and powerful blues voice.

We conclude this chapter with the familiar journey made in the 1940s by Muddy Waters and the first Sonny Boy Williamson; then, in the 1950s, by a stream of musicians including the second Sonny Boy (once the coast was clear) north to Chicago. Although Robert Johnson did not live to make that journey, he traveled there in spirit in the music of Elmore James, one of the most powerful, visceral, and stylus-rattling of all bluesmen, born in Richland, Mississippi on 27 January 1918. James's calling card, re-recorded many times throughout his career, was his slashing version of Johnson's 'Dust My Broom', and this established the distinctive mature James style: an open-tuned guitar fretted with a steel "bottleneck", punctuating each passionate lyric line and pumped through the amplifier as loud as possible. But if that sounds like a recipe for the inanities of "heavy metal" it would be to ignore the spaces that James left in his music, the marvelous sense of light and shade, the reverberating bass-string slides, and a voice wringing every dribble of passion from the lyric without quite losing control.

blues

john lee hooker

In November 1948 John Lee Hooker went into a Detroit recording studio with his electric guitar and four tunes. He came out with his first hit, 'Boogie Chillen'. Although Hooker has always credited his stepfather, Willie Moore, for being the inventor of the "Hooker" sound, the older man never recorded; and on disc, at least, nothing quite like 'Boogie Chillen' had been heard before.

While still only in his twenties – the record books claim he was born on 22 August 1917, although Hooker insists it was 1920 ("I lied about my age to get into the army... the ladies like a uniform") – the basic elements of Hooker's style are already there: the rhythmic guitar drone; a throbbing boogie punctuated by stabbed clusters of "seventh" notes; his willingness to provide percussion with his foot if no band is available; the brooding, meditative singing occasionally betraying the stutter in his conversational voice; and a total disregard of the traditional twelve-bar structure and rhyming couplets. As all his subsequent backing musicians have soon learned, Hooker goes with the flow of feeling rather than with the conventions of composition, and the feeling is so intense, so well-conveyed, that Hooker is a giant of the music, probably the most famous bluesman of all time.

John Lee Hooker was born on the Delta, in Clarksdale, Mississippi. He worked on Moore's nearby farm, accompanying his stepfather at local parties and dances before running away to Memphis at a very young age (eleven or fourteen

Far left: John Lee Hooker pictured here in the late 1940s. After his first recording sessions for the Modern label Hooker recorded for other labels using a variety of pseudonyms. In fact, it is estimated that between 1949 and 1953 Hooker made some seventy singles on twenty-four different labels using a dozen different names.

Left: Performing in Los Angeles in 1993. Hooker's career continues to go from strength to strength. "Success hit me by surprise," he explains, "but it didn't change me at all. I never thought I would be one of the greatest musicians alive..."

depending on whether Hooker is telling it). He then moved to Cincinnati, and by 1943 had arrived in Detroit where he worked in the city's car plants by day and bars by night. This led to those first recordings for the Modern label. His idol was the Texan master, T-Bone Walker, then the biggest star in Detroit. "He gave me my first electric guitar, from a pawnshop," remembers Hooker. At around this time legend has it that Hooker's fondness for "the ladies" almost led to a carbon-copy of Robert Johnson's death when he narrowly survived drinking a glass of laced whiskey.

By 1951 he had had three even bigger successes: 'Hobo Blues', 'Crawling King Snake' and 'I'm in the Mood'. Thereafter, he recorded for many labels, sometimes under cunning pseudonyms like John Lee Booker, and in the early 1960s became a hero of the British blues boom. Two of his songs in particular, 'Dimples' (1956) and 'Boom Boom' (1961) were in every rhythm and blues band's repertoire, and the latter title was a pop hit.

Hooker's own shrewdness has kept him largely free of the rip-offs that have ruined so many bluesmen. Moreover, he has never been short of work or hero-worship, often choosing to collaborate with white artists, like Canned Heat and Van Morrison. The unexpected happened in 1989 when, after several quiet years, his comeback album, *The Healer*, was a massive hit. The 1991 recording 'Mr Lucky', with Van Morrison and Ry Cooder in attendance, climbed almost to the top of the UK charts. Even by his own reckoning Hooker was in his seventies by then, the oldest pop star in British chart history.

But he was in no mood to retire. The 1995 album *Chill Out* betrayed no signs of weakening powers, just a supreme blues master who can attract backing musicians young enough to be his grandchildren. "I'm their idol," says Hooker by way of explanation.

the american renaissance

"Oh baby, don't you want to go
Back to the land of California
To my sweet home Chicago"

From 'Sweet Home Chicago' *by Robert Johnson*

Without underestimating the importance of the British blues revival of the 1960s, it would be misguided to imagine that the blues odyssey, which had started in the Deep South over a hundred years earlier, simply continued from Chicago to London before returning in the 1970s to enlighten a wider American audience. In fact, the musical legacy of the plantations continued to evolve in the ghettos of America's northern cities despite, rather than because of, the blues boom in the UK. Ironically, one of the leading figures in this development did indeed travel to London, but he did so as an innovative genius attempting to expand the language of electric blues rather than as a blues revivalist.

Jimi Hendrix's reputation may have suffered somewhat from two factors that he, being dead, could have no control over: one was that his revolutionary approach to the guitar became a blueprint for exponents of heavy metal, who were apt to explore the fretboard with volume but no feeling; the other was that his continued popularity has led to the release of every stoned improvisation that happened to be preserved on tape. Whereas Buddy Holly's doodlings are almost always intriguing – clear-headed and already well-formed – Hendrix was sometimes plain "out of it". Had he lived he would have had no truck with heavy rock, probably moving back toward his grounding in the blues, and he would surely have tried to ensure that unfocused recordings, never intended for public release, remained on the shelf.

Right: Jimi Hendrix, rock's most original and revolutionary guitarist. He had a natural feeling for the blues and much of his early work was profoundly blues-based.

When Hendrix hit British pop radio with his guitar sound on 'Hey Joe' and, even more emphatically, 'Purple Haze' in 1967, it was perhaps like hearing Robert Johnson when he returned from his wanderings. It was certainly like hearing Elvis, Little Richard, Jerry Lee Lewis, or Buddy Holly for the first time. This noise simply hadn't been made before.

James Marshall Hendrix was born in Seattle, Washington, on 27 November 1942 and worked in local bands as a teenager. He was left-handed, but simply learned to play a conventional guitar the wrong way round. By his early twenties he was touring as a backing guitarist to such prestigious artists as B.B.King, Little Richard, the Isley Brothers, and Ike and Tina Turner, before joining Curtis Knight and the Squires in the mid-1960s. He was later spotted playing the blues in a New York club by the Animals' bass player, Chas Chandler, and brought to England where he was teamed with drummer, Mitch Mitchell, and bass-player, Noel Redding, as the Jimi Hendrix Experience. They recorded 'Hey Joe' and Chandler has recalled that one record producer rejected it with the words, "I don't think he's got anything". The same company had turned down the Beatles.

The Jimi Hendrix Experience, like Cream, played in the "power trio" format, and, indeed, it was a promise that he would meet Eric Clapton that lured Hendrix to London. The Experience stayed closer to the blues than Cream, even though Hendrix took on board and developed the musical mood of the time. His second hit, the mould-breaking 'Purple Haze', was, in a sense, a psychedelic blues which linked blues technique and drug-induced imagery with guitar-effects like the wah-wah pedal. Once electricity had allowed blues guitarists to "sustain" a note (by expert control of feedback) Hendrix could make a "blue note" last indefinitely. As masterful tracks like 'Red House' proved, he could breath new life into the most conventional of blues patterns; but as his list of chart successes extended he produced variations on the theme: the reflective, restrained 'The Wind Cries Mary'; the gadget-driven 'The Burning of the Midnight Lamp'; a windswept, mythic version of

Dylan's 'All Along the Watchtower'.

Hendrix was the first black hero of the rock era. In between appearances at the Monterey Festival, where he turned the three chords of the Chip Taylor/Troggs hit 'Wild Thing' into quintessential Hendrix – and also bathed his guitar in lighter fuel before setting it ablaze – and Woodstock, where his savage, distorted version of 'The Star-Spangled Banner' was probably rock music's greatest-ever piece of political satire, he was tiring of the limitations of the Experience. However, his new group, Band of Gypsies, never quite recaptured that early magic, and he was rejoined by Mitchell for his final live appearance at the Isle of Wight Festival in 1970. Hendrix died on 18 September of the same year.

The record racks have continued to be filled by re-releases, re-packages and out-takes, and in 1994 a compilation album entitled *Blues* revealed once more where the roots of Hendrix's genius lay. It was a talent that owed little to the "blues renaissance", driven in America, as in Britain, mainly by white musicians, and one

Above: Johnny Winter at the Capital Radio Jazz Festival, Alexandra Palace, in 1979. In 1986 Winter became the first white artist to be inducted into the Blues Foundation's Hall of Fame.

Far left: Paul Butterfield, pictured in New York in 1974, two years after the demise of the Paul Butterfield Blues Band. Butterfield himself continued to perform sporadically throughout the 1970s but his two albums, released in 1976 and 1981, failed to resuscitate his fading career. He died in 1987 of a drug-related heart attack.

Above: Canned Heat touring in Germany at the height of their success in 1968. Three hit singles and a prestigious album would follow, but two years later Al Wilson's death reduced the band's potency.

tinued the American folk tradition; and later, in the dance clubs, where the full electrical charge of Muddy Waters was lovingly recreated.

Most of the practitioners, of course, like those in Britain, had not been near the kind of Chicago joint where Muddy was king, but this was not true of lawyer's son Paul Butterfield. He was a Chicagoan, born on 17 December 1942, who learned to play the harmonica in the rich style of Little Walter and then hung around in the right bars, eventually winning the approval of many of the black musicians to the point where he was even being invited to sit in with them. In 1965, three or four years after the distant London pioneers in the back rooms of their suburban pubs, he formed America's first white blues band of the rock era.

The image of the guitar hero – probably created above all by Eric Clapton's progress from the Yardbirds, to Mayall, to Cream – was perpetuated in the Butterfield band, and the best-known graduates were his original lead guitarist, Elvin Bishop, and his replacement, Mike Bloomfield, both of whom would leave, in turn, to form their own bands. When Bob Dylan controversially "went electric" in 1965, a symbolic moment when the two strands of revivalist blues came together, it was the Butterfield band who backed him – minus their leader, whose harmonica was surplus to requirements – and it is Bloomfield's guitar that can be heard on Dylan's most revolutionary achievements: the *Highway 61 Revisited* album and its epic hit single, 'Like a Rolling Stone'.

Meanwhile, back in the coffee houses of Greenwich Village, the Lovin' Spoonful – formed by New Yorker, John Sebastian, and taking their name from a Mississippi John Hurt song, 'Coffee Blues' – contributed, in 1966, to a groundbreaking "sampler" album on the Elektra label, *What's Shakin'*. Clapton played on three tracks – moonlighting from the Mayall band just before his final exit – and the album was a further stepping stone for the blues toward the developing rock mainstream.

But the growing white awareness of the blues was not, of course, confined to the east coast. In 1966 a graduate of the folk club circle in Austin,

suspects that Hendrix would have arrived at his unique style whether or not the blues had become fashionable.

The American revival developed on two fronts: firstly, in the folk clubs, coffee houses, and college campuses where the young white disciples of Son House, Leadbelly or Gary Davis (and sometimes the great originals themselves) played an acoustic blues that consciously con-

Texas, Janis Joplin, arrived in San Francisco looking for a blues band. Born in Port Arthur, Texas, on 19 January 1943, Joplin was blessed with a stunning blues voice: a full-tilt, rasping scream that could, in the space of a four-beat bar, become a tender, pleading whisper. As Whitney Houston was to prove so painfully in the early 1990s when she turned Dolly Parton's exquisite 'I Will Always Love You' into a vulgar, unmodulated screech, the one doesn't mean a thing without the other, although Houston's bank manager would probably disagree.

Joplin was the genuine article, a white blues singer, a disciple of Bessie Smith, and in Big Brother and the Holding Company she found a band who could support her changes of vocal gear. Their revival of Big Mama Thornton's 'Ball and Chain' at the 1967 Monterey Pop Festival was electrifying. Unfortunately though, Joplin was driven to live the whole legend of the death-wish blues singer – promiscuous, drug-addicted, hard-drinking – and she died of a heroin over-dose in 1970. However, the hits continued, most notably her chart-topping version of Kris Kristofferson's road song 'Me and Bobby McGhee', which was released posthumously, and the 1979 Bette Midler movie *The Rose* was inspired by Joplin's incandescent career.

Canned Heat were also on the bill at Monterey in 1967. However, whereas Joplin was most effective as a blues singer in a rock band context, Canned Heat were more purist, at least in their early days. They took their name from a Tommy Johnson song, and their repertoire was based on 1950s Chicago. The band was formed in Los Angeles in 1966 by Bob "The Bear" Hite and Al "Blind Owl" Wilson, from California and Boston respectively. As vocalists they were as contrasting as they were in appearance, with the bearded, overweight Hite singing in a rasping

Below: Steve Miller at the Knebworth Jazz Festival in 1974. Miller began playing guitar at the age of four under the auspices of Les Paul and T-Bone Walker who were both friends of his father.

bellow and the slim, bespectacled Wilson in a studious falsetto. Their biggest hits, from 1968 to 1970, were the delicate country blues 'On the Road Again' and 'Going Up the Country', and the churning Wilbert Harrison r&b classic 'Let's Work Together'.

When rock music began to get a little pompous in the late 1960s, the downhome boogie of Canned Heat, together with the exhilarating country-rock of Creedence Clearwater Revival, were life-saving blasts of rock 'n' roll sanity. But it couldn't last: Wilson died, lying in a back yard in a drug-induced coma, in 1970, and although the band has soldiered on through endless personnel changes ever since, Hite's death in 1981 finally broke the link with its early and most successful days. Hite was a true enthusiast for the blues and had built up an unrivaled collection of seventy-eights charting the early decades of the music. Unfortunately it was stored in California, a state straddling a fault line and prone to earth tremors. One does not have to be a record junkie to feel a chill at the image of Hite, arms outstretched, desperately trying to prevent his priceless, fragile shellac from smashing to the floor as the shelves of his vast storehouse shook.

White blues guitarists do not come any whiter than the albino Johnny Winter. Born in Leland, Mississippi, on 23 February 1944 and growing up in Texas, he first recorded in 1959 as a member of a teenage band before traveling to Chicago as an eighteen-year-old where he played with Mike Bloomfield, among others. In his mid-twenties he was back in Texas fronting a blues trio. The late 1960s saw the birth of the modern rock era, as distinct from pop, and Winter became its most famous straightahead bluesman when he signed with the Columbia label for what was then an unprecendented advance of $300,000.

In his early recordings Winter combined an urgent, snarling vocal delivery with striking technical virtuosity on guitar displayed at rock-festival volume, his repertoire drawing on Chicago and Texas blues. Although in the early 1970s he moved more toward heavy rock – before dropping out of sight for a while due to

drug addiction – he began to work with Muddy Waters in 1977 and subsequently helped to resurrect Waters' career. In the last years of his life the veteran recorded for Blue Sky, the same label as Winter, with the younger man acting as producer and guitarist. Having suffered a serious car crash, Waters was by this time performing while seated on a stool, concentrating more on his singing than guitar-playing, but, all the same, he remained a charismatic presence on stage, and the occasional little flurry of slide guitar was still worth waiting for. Meanwhile, Winter has also collaborated frequently with his younger brother Edgar, another powerful blues guitarist.

A further act who found fame at the Monterey Festival was the Steve Miller Blues Band. Miller, born in Milwaukee, Wisconsin, on 5 October 1943, worked in Chicago in the mid-1960s before moving to the West Coast where he was reunited with fellow guitarist, Boz Scaggs – they had started playing together before they reached their teens. The Miller band recorded with Chuck Berry in 1967, but following their success at Monterey the "Blues" tag was soon dropped. Although the blues has always been at the root of Miller's fluent, inventive guitar style his biggest success was the massive 1973 hit 'The Joker', a humorous, relaxed, mainstream song that reached the top of the UK charts in 1990 having been used on a TV commercial.

The blues baton was picked up by the J Geils Band, a Boston outfit formed in 1967 from two local groups, the J Geils Blues Band and the Hallucinations. Although they took a hard-rock approach to the music they always mixed classic blues in with their own songs: Otis Rush and John Lee Hooker were represented on their first album, released in 1970, and two years later they recorded with Buddy Guy and Junior Wells. Unusually for this turbulent era – from the recruitment of keyboard player Seth Justman in 1968 to the departure of vocalist Peter Wolf in 1982 – the band's personnel remained the same; and although it didn't last very much longer, in the 1990s guitarist J Geils and harmonica player Magic Sam were reunited in another blues outfit.

Left: Peter Wolf, the charismatic vocalist of the J Geils Band, pictured in 1982. Formed in 1969, the group was first discovered by Atlantic Records on a bill with Dr John, from which point they developed into one of America's premier live acts, presenting a high energy fusion of rock 'n' roll, blues and rhythm and blues.

At the same time as the J Geils Band were beginning to make a reputation in Boston, back down south a "southern boogie" form of white blues was developing. It is noticeable that the great studios and record labels of the "deep soul" era, operating in the heart of the segregated South, were, if anything, more racially integrated than comparable operations elsewhere (Tamla Motown in Detroit, for example, remained almost exclusively black), evidence surely that the white country guitar licks and songwriters working in the South helped to give southern soul at least some of its distinctiveness. In Memphis the house band at the Stax label, Booker T and the MGs, was made up of white guitarist Steve Cropper, white bass player Donald "Duck" Dunn, black drummer Al Jackson and black organist Booker T Jones; and at the Muscle Shoals studio in Alabama, where Percy Sledge took songs by white writers and turned them into classic soul, the session players included white guitarist Duane Allman.

Nashville-born Duane and his brother Gregg formed the Allman Brothers Band in 1968. Duane's lead guitar lines were twinned with those of Richard "Dickie" Betts, while vocalist Greg played keyboards. The group was the culmination of a lengthy apprenticeship for both

Right: Stevie Ray Vaughan, whose inspiring live performances rekindled public interest in the blues during the 1980s, pictured in New York in 1987, three years before his untimely death.

Left: The Fabulous Thunderbirds in Memphis, 1987. Like Stevie Ray Vaughan, the T-Birds played a key role in the blues renaissance of the 1980s. As well as producing their best-selling album, *Tuff Enuff,* 1986 also saw them win a W.C.Handy award for best blues band.

brothers, together and apart, and was almost instantly successful. The twin-guitar blues workouts became one of the distinctive festival sounds of the late 1960s, but it was not to last. By grisly coincidence, both Duane and bass-player Berry Oakley died in motorcycle accidents, in 1971 and 1972 respectively, and the distinctiveness of the early years was inevitably lost. Greg Allman has continued both with solo projects and versions of the "Brothers" band into the 1990s, however, and the latest reincarnation does include four of the original group. Greg may well still have much good music to reveal, but the distinctiveness of the Brothers band was very much of its time, another exhilarating variation on the "white blues" theme, and, sadly, it died with Duane.

However, another "white blues" innovation was brewing further west, in Austin, Texas. In 1975 singer and harmonica player Kim Wilson, bassist Keith Ferguson, guitarist Jimmy Vaughan, and drummer Mike Buck (later replaced by Fran Christina) formed the Fabulous Thunderbirds. Their self-titled debut album had to wait until 1979, by which time they had been seasoned by years of club work and had developed a rich and energetic version of up-to-date Texas blues. Their main song-writer, Wilson, showed a short lifetime's devotion to the blues, and original numbers were inter-laced with such respectful covers as Slim Harpo's 'Scratch My Back'. The album sleeve contained the boast "Girls Go Wild" and the image was of street-corner wise guys cranking out pumping blues songs between games of pool.

There followed several personnel changes – including Fran Christina – between the Thunderbirds and a Rhode Island nine-piece who had been together since the late 1960s, Roomful of Blues. With guitarists Duke Robillard and Ronnie Earl in the ranks, Roomful of Blues was closer to the "swing" blues style than the out-and-out rhythm and blues of the Thunderbirds. They even achieved the distinction of playing with Count Basie in 1974 as well as working with B.B.King, Lucky Millinder, J.B. Hutto, and the white Texan bluesman, Delbert McClinton, among others.

Ten years after the Thunderbirds started playing together – twenty years after the Allmans – there was another revival of interest in the blues among white record buyers in America which created a star in Seattle guitarist Robert Cray (see Profile on page 126). However, to many, the most talented player of the day was Jimmy Vaughan's brother, Stevie Ray Vaughan, who was born in Dallas on 3 October 1954. Moving to Austin to join his brother, the younger Vaughan played in a band that eventually became Stevie Vaughan and Double Trouble (named after a 1958 Otis Rush number). They made their recorded debut in 1983 with the album *Texas Flood*, which confirmed that Vaughan had synthesized influences both from the blues masters and more recent experimentation by blues-based rock bands from the 1960s like Cream and the Jimi Hendrix Experience.

However, there was a solid enough basis in pure blues amid the adrenaline rush of Vaughan's style for him to gain endorsements from both John Lee Hooker and B.B.King; just as Muddy Waters had invariably professed himself to be an Eric Clapton fan. (It is noticeable that the blues greats have always displayed color-blindness when assessing an ability to play the music with soul, although no doubt this is partly in recognition of the fact that it has often been the white stars who have opened commercial doors for the original masters.)

In the mid-1980s Vaughan struggled with drug addiction, but his 1989 comeback with the *In Step* album was hugely impressive and re-established his version of the blues in the charts. However, Vaughan died in a helicopter crash in 1990 returning home from a gig. He had just recorded with his brother Jimmy, and the resulting album *Family Style* was yet another hit. Although Stevie Ray Vaughan's career was sadly cut short, he will surely be remembered as one of a handful of great white exponents of the blues who have kept nudging the music back into the commercial mainstream.

John Hammond brings this chapter full circle as a white blues guitarist of stunning virtuosity who has always stayed faithful to the heart of the music, and who has straddled the two worlds of the acoustic folk club and the electric concert stage. His father, John Hammond Senior, was a legendary a&r man and record producer whose achievements span much of the century: he produced Bessie Smith and Billie Holiday in the early 1930s, and thirty years later, as an executive for the Columbia label, he played a crucial role in making it the leading imprint of the rock era. Hammond Senior's signings included Bob Dylan (known as "Hammond's folly" by unconvinced colleagues) and Bruce Springsteen. His son was born in New York in 1942, learned guitar and harmonica while at college, and began to play the country blues in the coffee houses of Los Angeles and Boston.

His reputation was established in 1963 with the release of his first, eponymous album on Vanguard, the leading label of the day for folk-blues music, and an appearance at the Newport Folk Festival. He played with members of the Band in the mid-1960s, first as a backing group to Canadian rockabilly legend, Ronnie Hawkins, and then as part of Bob Dylan's electric band. Other collaborators included Jimi Hendrix and Duane Allman, and in 1973 he formed an intriguing alliance with Mike Bloomfield and Dr John, a collision of white blues styles that produced a successful album in *Triumvirate*.

Hammond has continued to record regularly, and in the early 1990s signed to the British label Virgin for the impressive album *Got Live If You Want It*. It showed his distinctive style to good effect, using a bottleneck and vamping harmonica to give an irresistible percussive drive to the songs delivered in a rich, gravelly voice and with lyric lines punctuated by virtuoso guitar licks. Within weeks of launching the album in a small London club, Buddy Guy was on the same stage with his latest offering, confirming that the blues entered the final decade of its first century in excellent heart.

Left: John Hammond Junior, pictured here in New Orleans in 1994, started playing country blues in the late 1950s since when he has remained doggedly faithful to the genre. Having spent the early part of his career playing with other bands and blues offshoots, he established himself as a solo artist in the mid-1970s. Today, he continues to the fly the flag for traditional country blues both on record and in performance.

blues

PROFILE

muddy waters

Above: Muddy Waters in 1957, nearing the end of the decade that saw him rise from celebrity only in the Chicago clubs to become one of the most popular blues singers in the world in the 1960s.

The recordings made by Muddy Waters in Chicago in the late 1940s and early '50s form the most striking musical bridge between Delta blues and the birth of Chicago rhythm and blues. Many of the song lyrics look back over that bridge: 'I Feel Like Going Home'; 'Train Fare Home'; 'Down South Blues'; 'Louisiana Blues'. He is still more likely to sing of a catfish than a car factory, and on these early Chicago sides usually performs solo, or with the simplest instrumentation.

But the guitar is an electric one, the strings whipping and whining against a steel "bottle-neck", and gradually the backing builds, until by

1954 the greatest band in the history of the blues finds itself in the recording studio: Muddy on guitar and vocals, Jimmy Rogers on second guitar, Little Walter on peerless harmonica, Otis Spann on piano, Willie Dixon on bass, Fred Below on drums. Thereafter, the personnel varied from session to session, gig to gig, but that nucleus of the Muddy Waters Band epitomizes the hard drive, the musicianship, and the excitement of Chicago rhythm and blues. By this time Big Bill Broonzy was playing his acoustic guitar to white audiences and Muddy was king of the Chicago clubs.

McKinley Morganfield, probably nicknamed for his childhood habit of playing in the nearby creek, was born in Rolling Fork, toward the southern tip of the Mississippi Delta, on 4 April 1915. He grew up further north near Clarksdale and by his late teens was working locally as a musician on harmonica and guitar. In 1941 the folklorist Alan Lomax, who was building the Library of Congress Archive of Folk Song, recorded Muddy on a field trip to the Stovall plantation near Clarksdale and again a year later when he was accompanied by a band led by violinist Son Simms.

The move to Chicago came in 1943. Among those he came to know and work with were Broonzy, John Lee "Sonny Boy" Williamson and Eddie Boyd. His band started in 1947 as a trio with Jimmy Rogers and Little Walter, and they were first recorded for Aristocrat, forerunner of Chess. In the next ten years Muddy Waters pioneered Chicago rhythm and blues as an urban,

electric, club-based blues with its roots in the Delta, one of the most distinctive of all blues styles. In the ghettos of the industrial North, his music never quite kicked the southern mud off its boots, and it is this tension that gives his blues so much of its power. His catalog included 'I Can't Be Satisfied', 'Rollin' and Tumblin'', 'Hoochie Coochie Man', 'I Just Wanna Make Love To You', and 'Got My Mojo Working'; and was largely written by Willie Dixon.

His first tour to Britain in 1958, and above all his European tours in 1963 and 1964, established Waters as the main influence on the blues revival, and this led to far wider appreciation in America than had formerly been the case. In the 1970s his career was revived by Johnny Winter, and in the last years of his life he was recognized as the founding father of modern blues: he had presided in spirit over all the developments in the blues in both Britain and white America from the early 1960s onwards. Muddy Waters died at home in Chicago on 30 April 1983.

Above: Muddy Waters juicin' them blues at the Capital Jazz Festival, Alexandra Palace, 1979 just four years before his death. He remained active on the international music scene almost to the end.

the blues today and tomorrow

"The blues got after me
They ran me from tree to tree
They had me begging
Blues, please don't murder me"

From 'First Time I Met the Blues' *by Little Brother Montgomery,*
recorded by Buddy Guy

It is some time since Buddy Guy sang the number that brought him his first hit in 1960. "It's a young man's song," is how he describes its primal scream and its manic vocal and guitar gymnastics. His description shows rare integrity – ironically, because the mature Guy undoubtedly still has the power and vocal ability to do justice to 'First Time I Met the Blues', but he will no longer sing it on principle. Once described by Eric Clapton as "by far and without doubt the best guitar player alive", Guy carries our blues journey from the deep South – in his case Louisiana (and the South comes no deeper) – to Chicago, on to Europe, and up to the present day.

George "Buddy" Guy was born in Lettsworth, Louisiana, on 30 July 1936, the son of share-croppers. Although his parents did not have a radio when he was a child he was attracted by the guitars in a mail-order catalog. He told Scott Spencer of *Rolling Stone* magazine, "One year my dad had a good year, raised a lot of cotton and about broke even", as a result of which Buddy was given a two dollar guitar. Maybe they got a radio as well because he recalls hearing a John Lee Hooker song and persisting until his fingers found the right places on the fretboard to reproduce the riff.

Right: Buddy Guy in New Orleans, 1996.
In the 1970s and '80s Guy relied for his living on live performances – his spontaneity made him a natural performer.

Right: Delta bluesman Hound Dog Taylor was a compelling slide guitarist. Although he moved to Chicago in 1942 he did not become a full-time musician until the late 1950s, and his recording career did not really take off until he was signed to Alligator in 1971. He recorded three albums before his death in 1975 but it is as a rivetting bar performer that he is best remembered.

In 1957, after an apprenticeship in Baton Rouge that saw him playing with the area's big names, Lightnin' Slim, Lazy Lester and Slim Harpo, he went to Chicago in search of work. "I didn't move until I was twenty-one," he once told me, "because you couldn't get into bars before that." He went on to say that someone had heard him busking a Jimmy Reed tune and had introduced him to Muddy Waters, although *Rolling Stone* have published a slightly more dramatic version of events: "I was going on my third day without food... this guy [Muddy Waters] walks up to me... and sees the guitar, and he asks me, "Can you play the blues on that damn thing?" Waters then accompanied Guy to a bar where he listened to him play Guitar Slim's classic Louisiana blues, 'The Things I Used To Do', before taking him home and announcing to his wife, "Get dressed. We're going out. I got a little nigger here who can wear that guitar out!"

At first Chess passed on Guy – even when he beat Otis Rush, Magic Sam and Junior Wells in a "Battle of the Blues" contest at the Blue Flame Club – and instead he found a musical home on the West Side with Sam and Rush on the Cobra and Artistic labels. However, Willie Dixon brought him back to Chess in 1960 and 'First Time I Met the Blues' was the result, followed in 1962 by another rhythm and blues hit in 'Stone Crazy', a similarly impassioned performance. On Chess, however, royalties sometimes failed to reach the artist, and Guy kept his day job in a garage until promotor Dick Waterman teamed him with harmonica player Junior Wells in 1967. He took a two-week vacation from his job (a vacation from which he would never return) and set about developing the partnership that would flourish throughout the 1970s.

In Guy's early Chicago days there were as many as fifty clubs at which a newcomer could audition for work, sometimes in the "battles" that awarded a booking to the winner. As these clubs started to close down Guy bought his own, now called Buddy Guy's Legends, thereby assuming the responsibility of keeping the flame of Chicago blues burning. The 1991 album *Damn Right I've Got the Blues*, cut in London, together with a starring role in Eric Clapton's annual blues nights at the Albert Hall in London, prove that Guy remains as charismatic a performer as ever. His humor shows in his acute impersonations of other blues greats and his dynamism in the use of "pin-drop" silence to contrast with blistering flurries of notes. He remains the living master of Chicago blues.

To which Otis Rush would remind you that he, too, is very much alive and touring. Rush was born in Philadelphia, the one in Mississippi that is, on 29 April 1934 and moved to Chicago at the age of fourteen. By the mid-1950s he had his own group and was billing himself as Little Otis. His first session for Cobra was in 1956 before Magic Sam or Buddy Guy arrived at the label's storefront premises. With Willie Dixon on bass he announced himself as a remarkable and individual performer from the very first cut of Dixon's 'I Can't Quit You Baby'. In doing so he laid the ground rules for the so-called West Side style (referred to in the chapter "Chicago Plugs In"), discarding the rural Delta blues espoused by the Chess label on the other side of town in favor of a treble-heavy, acidic guitar sound as sharp as lemon juice, which used tremolo as a dramatic device able to support an impassioned, swooping vocal style (like a hyperactive Sonny Boy Williamson). The fact that Rush plays a conventionally-strung guitar upside-down and left-handed may have helped to color his style, giving a distinctive tone to his note-bending.

Rush was a local star by the time he added his guitar to Guy's first session in 1958. In the same year his final Cobra date produced two more classic blues, both written by Rush himself, in 'All Your Love' and 'Double Trouble'. In the early 1960s he moved to Chess, heightening his reputation with 'So Many Roads, So Many Trains', and then to Duke with 'Homework'. In 1969 Mike Bloomfield produced a comeback album (the first album, indeed, of Rush's career) called *Mourning in the Morning* which featured Duane Allman on guitar. He suffered more downs than ups over the next two decades, but all was not lost and he re-emerged as powerful as ever in the 1990s, in particular with 1994's album *Ain't Enough Comin' In* on the British label, This Way Up, which proved to be a warm-

Right: Lonnie Brooks, hitherto known as Guitar Junior, emanates from Dubuisson in Louisiana. He started as a backing guitarist for the celebrated "king of zydeco", Clifton Chenier, and in 1960 moved to Chicago where he starting recording and also became a popular club performer. He continues to record and perform.

ing confirmation of rehabilitated talent.

The triumvirate of living Chicago guitar legends is completed by Luther Allison. Whereas Guy journeyed north from Louisiana and Rush from Mississippi, Allison was born across the river in Mayflower, Arkansas, on 17 August 1939. His musical start was made in a familiar way: "I made my first musical instrument when

I was seven years old. It was a broom wire nailed to the side of the house, which I fretted with a bottle." He was not much older when he joined a touring gospel group, and his family moved to Chicago when he was twelve. He spent most of the 1950s working in bands, first with his brother, Ollie Lee, and then with another of his brothers, Grant (the "Rolling Stones" was just

Above: Otis Rush is highly rated within blues circles as one of the great guitar stylists, but although he continues to record and perform, he has never quite achieved the following he deserves.

one of the many names they traded under).

Allison did not get the opportunity to record until 1967 when he was signed up by Delmark. In the early 1970s he became a regular at the Ann Arbor Blues Festival, and in 1974 was signed to the Detroit label, Motown, as unusual a step as Albert King's earlier alliance with the Memphis soul imprint, Stax. Allison has an intense, attacking guitar style and is a magnetic stage performer: indeed, while huge success on records has always eluded him, in the 1970s he established a worldwide touring schedule of festivals, concerts and club dates to match that of B.B.King. In 1996 he won five Handy Awards, (the blues world's equivalent of the Oscars) and, like Guy and Rush, his career has recently gathered momentum following a 1994 album *Bad Love*, confirming that the 1990s are seeing something of a blues revival built on the rockstar status of Stevie Ray Vaughan and the crossover appeal of Robert Cray.

Meanwhile, the spirit of Hound Dog Taylor, born Theodore Roosevelt Taylor in Natchez, Mississippi, on 12 April 1917, lives on in the few Chicago clubs like Legends that remain true to the music. Taylor, who died in the city in 1975, never had a hit record, and although he was a frequent performer on the festival circuit, including visits to Europe, it is as a bar bluesman with his group the House Rockers that he will be remembered. He was a vigorous exponent of slide guitar, opting for a cheap Japanese instrument, and he once said, "When I die, they'll say, "He couldn't play shit, but he sure made it sound good!"" He was better than that, of course, but he is a timely reminder that, whatever sociological import the blues may have, however many awards are bestowed on performers of the caliber of Luther Allison, its basic function is still to "raise a ruckus" on a Saturday night.

And there is no better pianist for a Saturday night than Johnnie Johnson, who contributed to all of Chuck Berry's hits and is still hammering away at the keyboard. He does not play like a bluesman: in fact he has said, "I consider myself a piano player, period." and listening to him on one of Berry's rock 'n' roll classics essaying zany

decorations at the top half of the keyboard it seems that the pianist is in a world of his own. However, it is soon apparent that these flights of fancy are the perfect foil for Berry's artful, structured songs and that they would be hugely weakened without them.

Johnson was born in Clarksdale, West Virginia, in the mid-1920s and arrived in St Louis in 1952 where he formed the trio that Berry was soon to join. The partnership lasted until 1973 and has been revived occasionally since, but late in life Johnson is now celebrated once again in his own right. When he cut his bluesy *Johnnie B Bad* album in 1990–91 for the American Explorer series on Elektra, Keith Richards and Eric Clapton were among the guitarists, and the Rolling Stone acted as coproducer.

In the sleeve note Johnson refers to sharing a bill with Johnny Copeland, who afterwards joked, "Don't never put me on the same stage as Johnnie Johnson... He just stole my whole damn show!" Copeland was born in Haynesville, Louisiana, on 27 March 1937. His early childhood was spent in Arkansas where he recalls hearing not just bluesmen like B.B.King and the second Sonny Boy but country music as well. In 1950 he moved to Houston, Texas, and learned to play guitar. As a young teenager he was in the resident band at a Houston club, Shady's, a vital apprenticeship because, as he recalls, "Everybody that came through Houston played there: T-Bone Walker, Bobby Bland, Junior Parker, Big Mama Thornton..."

Although Copeland has worked continuously as a touring and resident bluesman, for some time he experienced a "stop-go" recording career that saw him casting around for new markets and appearing sporadically on a succession of labels (recording Dylan's 'Blowing in the Wind', for example, and playing on soul revues with artists like Otis Redding). In 1977 he began a more stable relationship with the Rounder label, and in 1985 shared a successful "summit meeting" album *Showdown!* with Robert Cray and Albert Collins.

One of the Fabulous Thunderbirds' energetic cover versions was of a "dance craze" novelty

Left: Albert Collins was a dynamic guitarist in the Texas blues tradition who achieved greatest celebrity late in life, as he was the main influence on 1980s blues star Robert Cray. After his 1958 instrumental 'The Freeze' his sharp, treble-heavy sound was characterized as "ice cold", and was achieved by playing high on the fretboard with the strings tuned to a minor chord.

called 'The Crawl', a churning slab of Louisiana rock 'n' roll. It was originated by Guitar Junior, who has now reverted to his real name of Lonnie Brooks and who has brought another regional blues style into the 1990s. He was born on 18 December 1933 in Dubuisson, worked with the New Orleans accordian player, Clifton Chenier, in the mid-1950s, and first recorded for the Louisiana label Goldband in 1957. By 1960 he was in Chicago where he recorded with Jimmy Reed, and his career has been based largely in Chicago ever since.

A contemporary of Brooks, the powerful vocalist Little Milton (Milton Campbell), was born in Inverness, Mississippi, on 7 September 1934. By the early 1950s he was working in Memphis where he recorded for the Sun label with Ike Turner. By 1961 he was recording in Chicago on the Chess subsidiary Checker, following which he scored a string of rhythm and blues hits in the 1960s, beginning with 'So Mean To Me' in 1962. 'We're Gonna Make It' reached number one in 1965, and other successes included 'Feel So Bad' and Little Willie John's 'Grits Ain't Groceries'. A move to Stax, where he joined Albert King and a roster of other bluesmen including Little Sonny and Freddie Robinson, continued to deliver hits throughout the 1970s, and since then he has recorded fruitfully for Malaco. Working on the borderline between the blues shouter and the soul stylist, Little Milton's success in this field has been bettered only by Bobby "Blue" Bland.

Bland, born in Rosemark, Tennessee, on 17 January 1930, has also found the Malaco label instrumental in prolonging his career. He is one of the most sophisticated of blues stylists, comparable in spreading the appeal of the music with B.B.King, who, incidently, employed Bland as his valet in the late 1940s. One of the Beale Streeters along with King and Johnny Ace, Bland began to find solo success in 1957 on the Duke label with 'Farther Up the Road', the first of an almost unparalleled roster of r&b chart hits that lasted for two decades. In the mid-1970s he was reunited with B.B.King for two smoothly crafted albums for the ABC label, *Together for the First Time...Live* and *Together*

Again...Live. On Malaco he has continued into the 1990s, his style hedged in by rock on the one hand, soul on the other, as the most distinctive contemporary interpreter of mainstream blues singing.

The West Coast's most celebrated representative these days is Joe Louis Walker, born in San Francisco on Christmas Day 1949. He learned to play guitar at the age of fourteen and grew up in the Haight-Ashbury district of the city – the 1960s world capital of hippies, drugs and psychedelia. For a while he shared a flat with Mike Bloomfield – through whom met Jimi Hendrix – and formed a blues-rock band called Blue Train. In the mid-1970s, however, he quit playing the blues in favor of gospel: "I hooked up with the Spiritual Corinthians. We were together for ten years... With a gospel group, you had to know how to work a tune."

A 1985 booking at the New Orleans Jazz and Heritage Festival rekindled Walker's love of the blues, and he formed a new band, the Bosstalkers. Since then he has recorded with B.B.King among many others, and has released a series of increasingly impressive albums. Nineteen sixty-six's *Blues of the Month Club* on Gitanes/Verve, was produced by white soul guitarist, Steve Cropper, and showed Walker to be moving in the Robert Cray direction, a versatile virtuoso fashioning a contemporary version of the blues with soulful overtones. The Spiritual Corinthians provided the backing vocals.

One of those with whom Walker has recorded recently is the British-born blues guitarist of Lebanese parentage, Otis Grand. Somewhat unusually, Grand writes but does not sing, though his reputation is such that he can call on a number of blues stylists, including the Fabulous Thunderbirds' Kim Wilson and Curtis Salgado. Grand is a remarkable technician who has absorbed all the electric blues styles and fashioned them into something of his own, an inventor rather than simply a revivalist. Luther Allison is among those on his 1996 album *Perfume and Grime* on the Sequel label.

The distinctive blues of Louisiana lives on in the music of Larry Garner, who was born in New Orleans in 1952. Garner grew up in Baton

Left: Joe Louis Walker, whose career started in the blues clubs of San Francisco in the 1960s, turned to gospel music in the mid-1970s before returning to the blues a decade later with the album *Cold is the Night,* the first of five on the Hightone label. Now on Verve, and at ease with everything from gospel through soul to bottleneck blues, Walker is one of the new generation of bluesmen.

Right: Gary Moore, who
played in mainstream rock
bands Skid Row and Thin
Lizzy and then flirted with
heavy metal before coming
home to the blues.

Rouge where Buddy Guy served his apprentice-ship, playing guitar in a gospel group in his early teens before switching to rhythm and blues. His first opportunity to record came from the English blues label, JSP, and it was in Europe that his reputation was established: he now records, like Walker, for the French blues and jazz imprint, Gitanes, distributed by Verve. His 1995 album *Baton Rouge* is a swampy mixture of blues, soul and country.

The reputations of Walker, Grand and Garner have only been established in the last decade, but an Irish contemporary of theirs, Gary Moore, provided a link with the rock-blues of the late 1960s when he played in Skid Row, and later in Thin Lizzy with Phil Lynott. Moore was born in Belfast on 4 April 1952, and when he left Thin Lizzy in 1979 to go solo his sound at first edged away from the blues, moving toward heavy rock. But in 1990, with guest appearances by Albert Collins and Albert King, he made the album *Still Got the Blues*, a huge seller that brought him back to basics. He later recorded with B.B.King, and more recently he has played the blues with Jack Bruce and Ginger Baker in BBM, a Cream for the 1990s.

The blues is unlikely to die until popular music dies since the one is at the heart of the other. It may have booms but they are never followed by busts: instead the blues continues to bubble away, simply taking a step back from the com-mercial spotlight for a while. With veterans like Buddy Guy as charismatic as ever, and, above all, with younger men like Larry Garner and Otis Grand keeping the flame burning, it remains in safe hands.

The only worry is that, like the deep southern soul that grew out of the blues in the 1960s, its essence is not at ease with modern recording techniques. If the technology exists, there seems to be an irresistible temptation to use it. However, the blues does not thrive when it has been multi-tracked and then mixed down into a homogenous whole. When a fluffed note can be seamlessly removed from a take and replaced with a perfect twin, some intrinsic feeling is lost. Overdubs allow more and more options, further

and further from the true soul of the piece.

If Bo Diddley had begun to play his out of tune but riveting 'Before You Accuse Me' today, he would be stopped within a couple of bars. Moreover, if he had ignored the command, the tape would have been quietly binned anyway. If Jimmy Reed stumbled up to a studio door tomorrow, he would probably be told to go away until he sobered up, and the impulse to make music would die with the warm Dutch courage of the whiskey.

One of the most exciting micro-seconds in rock 'n' roll is the moment when Scotty Moore crashes into the second guitar solo of Elvis Presley's 'Hound Dog'. Surely at least one of his fingers is misplaced: the chord sounds as if it was played by jumping on to an amplified steel-spring mattress. One fears that today Moore would be asked to "drop in" the correct chord and a moment of unexpected magic would be lost. Somehow the new generation of bluesmen must find a way of making the potential of digital perfection work effectively for them, thereby helping to capture the spirit of the blues rather than masking it.

However, all is far from lost. One of 1996's most surprising and welcome albums was by Rufus Thomas, recorded when he was in his late seventies. Born on 26 March 1917 in Cayce, Mississippi, Thomas moved to Memphis when he was a child and has recorded for numerous labels there, as well as holding down his day job as the city's most celebrated deejay. His 'Bear Cat' for Sun in 1953 was followed in the 1960s by a veritable menagerie of hits: 1963 bought the biggest, 'Walking the Dog', which was covered by the Rolling Stones, and there followed 'Can Your Monkey Do the Dog', 'Do the Funky Chicken', and 'Do the Funky Penguin'. He recorded rap in the mid-1980s, and in 1992 returned to past glories, tongue as ever in cheek, with 'Do the Funky Somethin''.

In the mid-1930s, just like the great Ma Rainey before him, Rufus Thomas was a Rabbit Foot Minstrel touring the tent shows as a come-dian and tap-dancer. More than sixty years later he gave us the album *Blues Thang!* with which he has brought our blues odyssey full circle.

blues

robert cray

It would be too limiting to call Robert Cray a blues musician. Blues may be at the root of his music but he has explored several other related genres. However, while Cray may rarely crank out a straightforward twelve-bar boogie, or strum a southern lament, the blues still informs all that he does. "I don't call myself a blues player," he says. "If I was pushed I'd say the band plays blues and rhythm and blues. But then there's touches of rock. And soul. So, if possible, I don't describe us at all."

Cray was born in Columbus, Georgia, on 1 August 1953, but he had a somewhat rootless childhood on account of the fact that his father was a serviceman. His love of the blues took root at an early age: "When I was real young, before I was even a teenager, I played blues and r&b records around the house," he remembers, "Then I played piano and my father wanted me to be Ray Charles. But in 1965 I got a guitar, 'cos everyone else had one, and I started getting into all the things that were on the radio. It wasn't until my senior year in high school that I rediscovered all those old records..."

Ironically, it was the Beatles and the British "invasion" that stimulated this teenage interest before he returned to the blues. His main inspiration was Albert Collins, who Cray first saw in concert in 1969 and who "reminded me of an organ player like Jimmy McGriff, attacking the notes so hard." Now living in Eugene, Oregon, Cray formed his first band with his schoolfriend, the bass player Richard Cousins in 1974. They built a reputation, particularly on the western

seaboard, and Collins himself would hire the band to back him when he played in that part of the country.

In spite of this heaven-sent apprenticeship, Cray's mature guitar style owes little to Collins, who was born in Leona, Texas, on 3 October 1932. The older man's technique was famously "ice cold", with needle-sharp note clusters usually at considerable volume. Cray, influenced as much by soul music as by the blues, is an altogether a more mellow technician. His voice, too, lacks a rough edge, but his music is saved from blandness by his lyrics, often bleak, brooding and dripping with revenge.

Cray's first album *Who's Been Talkin'* (1979) was under-exposed because not long after its release the record company went bankrupt. In 1985 he made the album *Showtime!* with Albert Collins and Johnny Copeland which subse-

quently won a Grammy award. In the meantime his fourth and most successful record, *Strong Persuader*, which was released in 1986, became a million-seller and represented a rare showing for the blues in the American charts. Shortly before his mentor's death in 1993 Cray and Collins recorded together. Three years earlier the soul side of Cray's music had been stressed in 1990's *Midnight Stroll*, which featured the peerless Memphis Horns, Wayne Jackson, and Andrew Love who would later join the Robert Cray band.

If 1992's *I Was Warned* lacked grit, it was only a temporary disappointment: a year later *Shame and Sin*, with a powerful sense of anguish never far from the surface of the lyrics, provided ample proof that Cray could easily overcome the tendency to smother the feeling with immaculate technique.

Above: Seen here performing in New York in 1987, Robert Cray formed his own band in 1974, made his recording debut five years later, and is now the most celebrated of the younger blues-influenced guitarists.

Far left: Robert Cray started off by learning the piano but was inspired to take up the guitar when the Beatles hit America in the mid-1960s. He first saw his mentor Albert Collins playing in 1969 and turned to the blues.

INDEX

Picture and Song Credits

Front cover: T.Motion; back cover: Michael Ochs Archive/Redferns; half-title: David Redfern; 6–7: J.Marffy; 8–9: Frank Driggs Collection; 10: Frank Driggs Collection; 11: Glen Baker Archives/Redferns; 12,13: Frank Driggs Collection; 14: Max Jones File/Redferns; 16–17: David Redfern; 18, 19: Frank Driggs Collection; 20–21: Michael Ochs Archive/Redferns; 22: Corbis-Bettman; 24,25: Frank Driggs Archive; 26: David Redfern; 27: Michael Ochs Archive/Redferns; 28: Frank Driggs Collection; 29: Michael Ochs Archive/Redferns; 32: Library of Congress, USF34-40828-D; 34: Frank Driggs Collection; 35: William Gotlieb/Redferns; 36: Michael Ochs Archive/Redferns; 37: David Redfern; 38: Michael Ochs Archive/Redferns; 39: Frank Driggs Collection; 40: Brian Shuel/Redferns; 41: Alison Turner/Redferns; 42 43: Gert Schlip/Redferns; 44–45: Michael Ochs Archive/Redferns; 46: David Redfern; 47: Peter Symes; 48: Michael Ochs Archive/Redferns; 50: Michael Ochs Archive/Redferns; 51: David Redfern; 52: Mike Doyle; 53: Michael Ochs Archive/Redferns; 54: Max Jones Files/Redferns; 55: David Redfern; 56–57: David Redfern; 58: Sylvia Pitcher; 59, 60: Frank Driggs Collection; 61: David Redfern; 62–63: Sylvia Pitcher; 64–65: David Redfern; 66: David Redfern; 67: Glen Baker Archives/Redferns; 68: Andrew Putler/Redferns; 70: Michael Ochs Archive/Redferns; 71: Sylvia Pitcher; 72–73: Michael Ochs Archive/Redferns; 74: David Redfern; 75: Bob King/Redferns; 76: Sylvia Pitcher; 77: Finn Costello/Redferns; 80: Dick Barnatt/Redferns; 81: Sylvia Pitcher; 82–83: Pictorial; 84, 85: Sylvia Pitcher; 86–87: Sylvia Pitcher; 88: Michael Ochs Archive/Redferns; 89, 90, 91, 92: David Redfern; 93: David Redfern; 94: Glen Baker Archives/Redferns; 95: Henrietta Etherington-Smith/Redferns; 96, 97: Pictorial; 98: Frank Driggs Collection; 99: Pictorial; 100–101: David Redfern; 102, 103: David Redfern; 104: 105: Davis Ellis/Redferns; 107: Pictorial; 108: David Redfern; 109: Ebet Roberts/Redferns; 111: Leon Morris/Redferns; 112: Frank Driggs Archive; 113, 114–115: David Redfern; 116: Glen Baker Archives/

Redferns; 118, 119: David Redfern; 120: Mick Hutson/Redferns; 122: Marc Marnie/Redferns. 124–125: Dave Ellis/Redferns; 126: Pictorial; 127: Ebet Roberts/Redferns; end-papers: Sylvia Pitcher.

8:"Diddie Wa Diddie" (Davis) by kind permission of MCA Music Ltd; 20: "See That My Grave Is Kept Clean" (Blind Lemon Jefferson) by kind permission of MCA Music Ltd; 32: "Looking Up At Down" (Big Bill Broonzy) by kind permission of MCA Music Ltd; 45: "Good Rockin' Tonight" by Roy Brown © 1948 Fort Knox Music Co. Inc. and Trio Music Co. Inc. – lyric reproduced by kind permission of Lark Music Ltd. (Carlin), Iron Bridge House 3 Bridge Approach, London NW1 8BD; 56: "The Blues Had A Baby" written by Muddy Waters and Brownie McGhee © Watertoons Music administered for the world by Bug Music – lyrics used by kind permission. All rights reserved. International copyright secured; 72: "Can Blue Men Sing the Whites" words and music by Vivian Stanshall ©1968, reproduced by kind permission of EMI Music Publishing Ltd., London WC2H 0EA; 86: "Walkin' To New Orleans" (Antoine "Fats" Domino, Dave Bartholomew, Robert Guidry) by kind permission of International Music Publications; 100: "Sweet Home Chicago" words and music by Robert Johnson. International copyright secured. © King of Spades Music. Words reproduced by permission of Interstate Music Ltd and Paul Rodrigues Music Ltd; 114: "The First Time I Met the Blues" (Little Brother Montgomery) by kind permission of Warner Chappell.

Note: Every effort has been made to contact original sources, where known, for permissions. The captioning of all the illustrations in this book has been the responsibility of Salamander Books Ltd., and not the author.